White WATER

Navigating the rapids of church conflict

Bill Elliff

WHITEWATER
Navigating the Rapids of Church Conflict

By Bill Elliff

Published by TruthInk Publications
6600 Crystal Hill Road
North Little Rock, Arkansas 72118

Design by Keith Runkle

ISBN: 978-0-615-40308-3

Printed in the United Sates of America

Dedicated to my wife, Holly,

my greatest counselor, encourager, and partner

in the ministry God has privileged us to share.

TABLE OF CONTENTS

INTRODUCTION

Churches have conflict because they're filled with people who are human and sinful and opposed by a devil who is devious and strong. If you have not encountered conflict in the church, then either…

- you've not reached the flash point yet,
- the church is not growing and progressing, or,
- someone before you fought the battle so you could build.

Nobody prepares us for this. There are great books and seminars on how to grow a church, manage people, develop teams in a church, reach the community. But very few church leaders are armed with the resources to navigate the whitewater of congregational conflict.

Conflict is the greatest test of leadership. It's also the most significant opportunity for growth. Most great advances have come out of such difficulty. The cross was all about conflict. When properly managed, it can be your friend and not your enemy. It can be leveraged and great progress gained for the glory of God. But, you must know how to respond.

This book was borne out of multiple experiences as a pastor and also hundreds of hours of counseling pastors who have faced conflict in leading their churches forward. It is designed as a tool to give church leaders hope, direction, and confidence to "shepherd the flock of God among you."

In professional whitewater slalom racing (an Olympic sport), each kayak must go through certain "gates" or they will be disqualified. At the end of each chapter there is a "Navigational Gate" that will give you a practical step of application. Although these are short, they are powerfully important. Take time and work through them carefully. You may discover these practices will save you from spiritual, emotional, and even physical disqualification.

If you've not faced your moment of crisis, just keep breathing. It's coming and how you navigate it will determine both your future and the future of those you lead. Rightly handled, conflict can be the single greatest tool to help you break through to new levels as a leader and see the church progress for the glory of God.

Bill Elliff
Maumelle, Arkansas
August, 2010

AMBUSHED

Matt Johnson collapsed in the chair. The Sunday newspaper was on the table beside him, but he was just too tired to pick it up. He flipped on the television to try and escape the twin demons of hopelessness and fear that seemed to be perched on each shoulder.

"How did this happen?" he thought.

It had been just a few short years ago when he drove onto the parking lot of his new church. The air was crisp that November morning and he remembered sitting in his car with tears in his eyes, overwhelmed with a sense of destiny.

His wife, Sharla, was thrilled with the city. It had a great blend of old town feel and new town conveniences. Their house was beyond their imagination, even though it was going to be a stretch financially. All three of his kids made good friends within the first two weeks. The people overwhelmed them with love and support, even filling their shelves with food the day they arrived.

Matt quickly and effortlessly connected with some of the young leaders. James Lewis appeared to be the kind of man that would not only be a great leader, but a good friend. In fact, most of the young men were amazingly hungry to grow. The thought of living life with these men made Matt smile every time he thought about it.

Every corner of the church and city had seemed loaded with potential. The university located two miles from their campus was filled with thousands of students who needed Christ. Even before he arrived, God began to flood Matt's mind with ideas about how to reach and equip hundreds, maybe thousands of students. How awesome it would be if there could be a movement on that campus for Christ! Their church could literally become a sending station for the world.

But it wasn't just the younger men and students that Matt engaged. Hattie Jenkins, the oldest lady in the church, wrote him a nice note voicing her support. In fact, all the people seemed overjoyed. Matt received dozens of emails and phone calls from every age group telling him their excitement about his vision. The search team that called him said the church was ready for whatever change he would bring. He was filled with new ideas and fresh insight and felt the smile of God upon his decision to accept this assignment.

Matt dreamed of planting his life here. This had all the potential to be his most effective ministry—maybe even his primary life's work—his unique contribution to the Kingdom of God.

It didn't take long for the church to begin to grow. Matt was a passionate communicator, good strategic thinker, and a faithful pastor. Sadly, there was a vacuum of good preaching and authentic ministry in the city. Very quickly the word spread about the new pastor and the church began to accelerate. A record number of visitors attended their weekend services. Matt had dreamed of a church of genuine community, powerful worship, and consistent external focus. Each month more changes were put in place and with each successive change the church gained more momentum. Two years went by quickly.

That was why Matt was so surprised when John Griffen and a few of his old buddies invited him to lunch. Matt was a man's man and the men's group he had started was one of the most exciting venues of ministry. But John and his friends, who had been leaders in the past, never really engaged with that group. Matt really didn't know these men well. As John came by to pick him up at the church Matt wondered why he had called.

He soon found out as they pulled into the local café. After ordering "the usual" John and his buddies told Matt what they were hearing.

"Pastor, we really appreciate you. That message you gave on how to handle our problems two weeks ago was really good. But a lot of people," John said, "are concerned that we're moving a little too fast."

The men started slowly, but voiced their concerns with increasing speed over the next thirty minutes. Matt realized he hadn't eaten a bite of his food as he pushed his plate to the side. While looking at John, he had the odd realization that his appetite was completely gone. He asked a few questions to try to make some sense out of what these men were saying and listened attentively, writing a few of their comments on a napkin.

When one of the men took a short breath, Matt jumped in and reminded them of some of the good things God was doing, but it didn't seem to slow them down. As his coffee cooled off, he realized they did have a few valid concerns and unconsciously decided to believe the best about their motivations. He had to swallow hard a few times, but then remembered that good leaders need to be open to evaluation. As they shook hands to leave, Matt told them he'd think and pray through what they said and thanked them for their concern.

Matt turned the radio off on the drive home as he processed what had just happened. *"These guys are all right. It wasn't the most enjoyable moment of my life, but if you're going to be a leader, you've got to be ready to take a little heat,"* he thought to himself. But in his gut, something felt off key about the whole experience.

As he walked through the door at home, Sharla met him with a hug, but immediately sensed something was bothering her husband. She could always read Matt like a book. He sat down in his recliner and began to recount the men's comments, trying not to go into every detail so Sharla wouldn't be worried.

"I don't think it's a big problem. Change is hard and it's going to take them a little longer to adjust," he mused.

Sharla had another opinion. "Control," was her one word summary. "Don't you realize they're just trying to control you, Matt? They were in charge and they're losing their positions. I think there's more to this than you realize," she said. With his head he nodded agreement, but inwardly he knew Sharla just didn't understand the give and take of church leadership. Pastoring takes a lot of patience. But in the back of his mind, Sharla's comments attached a sticky note of doubt. As much as he hated to admit it, Sharla's discernment had trumped Matt's naïveté many times. He had the tendency to believe the best about almost anyone. It was one of his most endearing traits in some ways, but often made him clueless about people's underlying motives.

As the weeks wore on, her comments proved prophetic. Matt faced increased resistance from this small group who claimed to represent many others. Everything Matt proposed was now questioned and took longer and longer to push through to a decision. Progress slowed. In fact, Matt found himself diverting large amounts of sideways energy to questions that shouldn't matter. *"Why did we change the bulletin?" "The music is hurting my ears." "What authority does the youth pastor have?" "Why don't we have more regular business meetings?" "Your sermons aren't feeding us anymore."*

One afternoon he sat at his computer in deep frustration and began to write out his thoughts to try to make some sense of what was happening—to put his finger on what was bothering him.

Why did so many people have to sign-off on every decision? Were these the people who should decide the direction of the church anyway? When prayer meetings were called, they weren't there. When clear God-moments occurred, they didn't really "get it." Did they have the mind of God? Did they really understand better than he what it would take to move the church forward? To reach the next generation for Christ? Why did they have to control every decision? And who were "they" anyway?

The new people who had joined and a whole group of emerging leaders in the church really appreciated his leadership and greatly encouraged him. "We've needed this for a long time," James Lewis assured him. "In fact, if you hadn't come along, I don't know if we'd still be here. Life is short and Susie and I want our lives to make a difference. You're positioning this church and our lives to go there, Matt. Don't be discouraged and don't give up."

Matt discovered a real kindred spirit with these leaders. They were progressive, responsive to God, and had a genuine heart for ministry. They loved to worship. Matt found he couldn't out-challenge them. The more God called for, the greater they responded. They were willing to take risks and do whatever it would take for the kingdom to be advanced and God's reputation to be enhanced in the city. He knew a powerful, prevailing church could be built with this team.

The fall came and then the spring. Little battles were fought. Some were won, some lost, but Matt continued to believe God's vision could be fulfilled here. This was God's church! He would not abandon her. Surely all the members could agree on the need of reaching the lost and unchurched in the community. Anyone could see that what they had been doing in the past had been unproductive for years. Surely they would be open to new ideas and methods…the things he was learning as an aggressive pastor and student of the church. Surely they would become excited about the things that charged his heart and fueled his passion. Didn't they hire him to lead? Hadn't they assured him many times that, "we're behind you, Pastor"?

And then it happened. Matt never saw it coming, but it came nonetheless. It just didn't make sense because the issue was not that controversial. In fact, Matt and his leadership team had proposed other ideas that were more radical in the past which had been adopted, although grudgingly by some.

When it was discussed among the staff, they anticipated these new visionary steps would meet with some opposition just as others had. But they never dreamed the reaction would be so intense. Those who dissented acted like the passage of this proposal would bring the absolute demise of the church. In fact, John Griffen stopped by to make sure that Matt knew the gravity of the situation.

John sat down in the green leather chair in the pastor's study and leaned forward. Matt felt his whole body tense and his face twitched as it did occasionally when his adrenaline started pumping.

"Pastor, if you push this forward I believe you'll split the church. There are a lot of unhappy people. I've tried to calm them down, but if you press this initiative, I can't be responsible." John rambled on for half an hour. This time, Matt refused to let his accusations go unchallenged. Before John left, they were in a fairly heated discussion.

John left that meeting and spread the word about Matt's response. The staff began to hear all kinds of half-truths and outright lies filtering back. Matt knew that people who had seemed like real supporters were beginning to distrust him and speak against his leadership. He discovered John Griffen had a lot of followers—not because of his spirituality, but because of his long tenure in the church and his willingness to be the opposition leader and the spokesmen for others. Matt was surprised though at some of the people who opposed him and the directions they were proposing. These were people he had helped in times of crisis, ministering to their needs. Their rejection of his leadership hurt. Bad. In fact, it didn't feel like a rejection of his leadership. It felt like a rejection of him.

The gossip became intense. There had always been a measure of this kind of talk, but nothing like what occurred now. Accusations flew, rumors spread. Areas which were not even remotely related to the issues at hand began to be discussed among "concerned" members.

Matt spent several sleepless nights searching his heart before God to see if it was some sin he had committed, some leadership mistake he had made that ignited this conflict. Certainly he made errors and admitted them when needed. But the more he examined his heart, the more he felt a clear conscience regarding his leadership. Matt had not been perfect (who is?) but he had tried to lead with the right motivation. To the best of his knowledge, he had sought to obey God in his leadership with a balance of grace and truth.

It was so confusing. How could genuine Christians act like this? How could any believer not see the importance of changes that would reach more people?

So he sat in his chair this Sunday afternoon. Surrounding him was a city of hurting people who needed to see a church filled with the love of God. The church he thought would be his life work was in the inevitable path of a tsunami and he was caught in the undertow. The mission he had given his life to seemed impossible to fulfill.

How in the world could he navigate these rapids of church conflict?

From: Matt Johnson
To: Jim Bradford
CC:
Subject: Church problem

Dear Rev. Bradford,

A friend of mine encouraged me to write because he said that you had gone through some similar experiences. How that could be, I don't know. If it is true, I'm sorry, for I wouldn't wish this on my worst enemy.

I'm entering my third year at our church. I've never been in a place with so much potential. The need around us is great, but the longer I pastor this church, the more I am uncovering some serious dysfunctions. There is a tremendous aversion to change. I don't understand, really, how any genuine Christian could oppose the simple things we are trying to do, but I am finding major opposition developing everywhere I turn. In fact, I'm wondering if I can lead this church at all.

I don't know if I'm filled with faith, naiveté or wild optimism, but I feel like God wants to do something here. At this rate, though, we're not going to make the turn. Do you have any advice?

Thanks for taking the time to help,

Matt Johnson

- - - - - - - - - - - - - - - - - - - -

From: Jim Bradford
To: Matt Johnson
CC:
Subject: RE: church problem

Dear Matt,

I'm so glad you had the courage to write. I've heard about your work there and thrilled you felt the liberty to contact me.

A pastor is not only a shepherd, but a spiritual physician. All churches have diseases at times that endanger their health and make them unable to move forward. As a good physician, your first task is to put the stethoscope to the patient and diagnose the problem correctly.

Enclosed are some thoughts about how to make a proper diagnosis. Take time with this. If you miss the diagnosis you could spend a lot of time treating the wrong problem while your patient is dying on the table. (And we don't even want to talk about the malpractice issues!)

Don't hesitate to write, for my past experiences take on greater value as I am able to help young pastors like you.

And by the way...*just call me Jim!*

By God's grace,

Jim

CHAPTER ONE

Diagnosing Conflict

"What's the real issue?"

My oldest brother never waits to act and in most cases he has a real confidence that he knows what to do. I often say about Tom that he's "sometimes wrong, but never in doubt!"

Once he was on the final leg of an overseas flight when a man across the aisle slumped over his dinner tray and was unconscious. Tom quickly diagnosed that he was choking. The real reason he came up with this diagnosis was that he had recently watched a program on television about how to administer the Heimlich maneuver to choking victims. With his diagnosis firmly in mind, he quickly pulled the unsuspecting man out of his seat, wrapped his arms around him with his fists under his sternum, and popped him two or three times with great force to get the supposed obstacle out of his windpipe. Unfortunately, what Tom later discovered was that the man wasn't choking at all. He'd had a heart attack!

In this case, his attempts didn't hurt the man, but the Heimlich maneuver can cause serious injury. I suggested to Tom that if he wanted to continue as an armchair doctor he might need to watch some programs on malpractice lawsuits!

Misdiagnosis can be fatal. A doctor who calls a malignant growth benign not only misses the diagnosis, but also harms the patient. Every person will ultimately die regardless of the good services of a faithful doctor. But no doctor (or patient) wants an untimely death that could have been averted if the right diagnosis had been made and treatment given.

If you think being a doctor is a challenge, try being a church leader! The task of maintaining health in a volunteer group of sinful, hurting people who are constantly assaulted by the philosophies of the world and the deceptions of an enemy bent on their destruction takes a skilled spiritual physician. Diseases attack this Body inside and out. Compounding the problem is the fact that the pastors and church leaders themselves can be infected with the same ailments. How do we know if it's a problem with the congregation or with the leaders or both?

Most fatalities in church life are not caused by sudden, tragic collisions, but by long-term diseases that finally present themselves. Spiritual cancers can lurk under the surface and grow undetected. In fact, one of the enemy's greatest tactics is to actually "sow tares among the wheat"—lost men and women with no capacity for making spiritual decisions who are planted by the enemy to disrupt God's work (see Matthew 13:25-40).

Diagnosis is critical. Multiple repercussions can occur from a wrong analysis such as…

Superficial Healing. Treating only surface problems is like putting a band-aid on a cancer that will ultimately dominate and destroy.

Loss of Leadership Capital. Good leaders in the congregation could lose confidence in a leader who makes unwise assessments. In fact, it could lead to a premature departure from his ministry position.

Increased Complications. A wrong prescription could further complicate the problem while never resolving the foundational issue.

Loss of Leadership Development. The leadership growth that could have occurred to help face the next level of challenges can be lost.

Discouragement and Disenchantment. The lack of resolution could cause the pastor and leaders to become discouraged and hopeless regarding future change. Also, a pastor who fails at a leadership challenge can easily lose confidence in his own ability to lead, becoming tentative and fearful.

Strengthened Opposition. Those who oppose real progress (and may have opposed others in the past) could be strengthened in their control and resolve, creating a higher wall to scale for future leaders.

Poor Health and Lack of Growth. With a wrong diagnosis and treatment, the church will not get healthy. Growth will be stunted or stopped entirely. In fact, it could ultimately lead to the death of the church. A recent study by Andy McAdams stated that more than 2,000 churches close their doors every year and 1400 pastors leave their jobs every month!

Medical doctors spend many years and thousands of dollars to learn how to diagnose two primary things:

- What are the medical problems?
- How can we correct them?

Most pastors have received some training in how to bring healing to the primary personal problems of their church members, but very little help on how to diagnose and resolve the corporate problems that erupt. We fail to realize that corporate problems can paralyze a church and prevent it from any effective ministry to individual lives, both inside and outside the church. Satan knows this well. When conflict occurs in a local church, what's the problem?

Sometimes it's the PASTOR'S Fault

We would be foolishly proud to assume that there are not many occasions when the fault-meter points directly to the leader. It would make sense that Satan would seek to lure leaders into temptation and sin that would adversely affect the church. Sometimes the pastor is not sinful, but has just made some honest leadership mistakes. Some of the possible issues could be as follows:

Personal Sin. Unresolved anger, unholiness, moral impurity, lack of intimacy with God, laziness, financial mismanagement will always manifest itself through a leader's life. Paul told his young pastor friend, Timothy that, "deeds that are good are quite evident and those which are otherwise cannot be concealed" (I Timothy 5:25). A lack of integrity is good cause for people to question a pastor's leadership and should be properly confronted by the church.

Poor timing. Every leader is capable of moving too fast or too slow. Rushing a decision can cause good, godly people in the church to fear missing God's direction (*"We don't know if this is right, but he wants us to blindly follow."*). Letting the opportunity pass because of over-caution, passivity, or man fearing can cause strong, effective leaders to lose confidence in a pastor (*"He doesn't have the guts to make the tough calls and be decisive."*).

Inadequate training. Pastors are ill-equipped to handle many of their leadership challenges. If they knew better, they might do better. It is possible for a pastor to make a sincere leadership step that is sincerely wrong. Every pastor needs to hone his leadership skills. This takes some authentic humility that leads to a teachable heart, serious intentional study, conversations with godly mentors, and much time before God.

Improper strategy or structure. If a church leader doesn't properly assess his church, he may try to lead them to embrace initiatives that do not fit his people or his field. A mismatched strategy can create unnecessary conflict.

Poor or unbiblical structure that has been developed may be hindering communication or causing frustration. This may be structure the pastor helped create or it may be something he has inherited. In either case, at some point it should be realigned.

Ungodly motivations. Every pastor has dealt with a desire to succeed for the sake of success or personal fame. This is often fueled by an unholy desire to compete with other churches or gain recognition among colleagues. It is pure, godless pride that motivates a man to use the church to enhance his reputation.

Unnatural style. Often a young pastor has been mentored by an older leader who is vastly different in temperament and style. Or he goes to a conference, listens to a seemingly successful pastor and tries to emulate what he's heard. To fail to step up and do what his mentor did, or others have taught in some situations, may seem like a lack of courage.

What the young pastor fails to realize is that he must be his own man, develop his own style, and lead from his own unique temperament. Many have made leadership mistakes by trying to be someone they aren't. Although he may be doing what he thinks is right, this forced style will always lack authenticity and create problems.

Lack of Leadership Capital. Pastors don't get the opportunity to really lead simply because they have a job position. They may think they do, but they don't. Leadership is earned. If a pastor doesn't lead well before conflict arises he may find himself with a deficit of leadership equity. Wise pastors understand the value of developing this capital before tough issues are faced (and there are always some if you're going to lead a church). This is not preparation to manipulate people, but to lead well and faithfully in advance of crisis moments so people will follow in the midst of conflict.

Several factors can put leadership money in the bank for the emotional recessions that may occur during conflict.

Caring for people is important. When we don't know our sheep or how to tend to their needs, we are in trouble when we ask them for tough steps. Proverbs says we are to "know well the condition of our flocks and pay attention to our herds" (Proverbs 27:23). People who don't really know us will rarely follow us well.

Making wise smaller decisions and celebrating success is critical. This helps people see the value of change on a smaller scale and prepares them to follow when greater sacrifice is called for.

Being well prepared for every meeting is a must. Whoever is prepared in any meeting leads. If you are coming to the table and leading out of your hip pocket, you will gradually lose respect before others. If you are thoughtfully, prayerfully prepared before every meeting, but still open and sensitive to the ebb and flow of the Spirit, real leaders will recognize this and your capital will rise.

Involving others in decision-making is important. No pastor is infallible and he needs godly counselors around him that he can trust. Developing a pattern of the right kind of involvement with the right people helps others know they can trust that the pastor is not making decisions in a vacuum. The big plans he later proposes will be more readily accepted.

Listening to others is a visible mark of humility. If the people around a pastor sense that he is so proud that he never pays attention to others, always has to have his own way, interrupts everyone else's sentences, takes credit for what others have done, has to be recognized, or is defensive when corrected, his credibility will degenerate quickly! Godly people don't follow proud pastors.

But perhaps the greatest key is to capture the hearts and minds of the men of your church. I believe developing male leadership is critical to a healthy church. Anything and everything that can be done to gradually help these men come to biblical convictions about the church, God's mission, and the needs of the world around them is vital.

Once, when facing a big challenge in a church, I realized that good men didn't understand where we needed to head. This was not their fault, it was mine. I was their leader. We began an early morning men's training time and to my surprise 110 men showed up. For about four months we studied the real needs of the next generation, the ineffectiveness of the church currently, and what must be done to correct this.

One morning in particular turned the tide. We studied a statistic by Thom Rainer from his book, *The Buster Generation,* which stated the evangelization rates for American evangelical churches over the last 50 years.

Birth	% of people evangelized by the church
Before 1951	65%
1951-1964	35%
1965-1977	15%
1978-1994	4%

I will never forget the moment when we saw that last statistic. The room went strangely silent and then I heard men begin to weep. All across the room there was a sobering awareness that if we continued to do the same things the same way, 96% of our children's and grandchildren's generation would not know Christ. That statistic alone served to bring about significant change. By God's grace, I was leading them to see what needed to be understood. Not only did this get us there, it gave me tremendous leadership capital among these men. We had the cavalry to charge the hill.

If a pastor is guilty of some of the preceding issues (or other faults God brings to his mind) and it has contributed to the conflict, he has to be humble enough to admit it honestly. Usually a pastor doesn't need to accept 100% responsibility for the problem. But he must always have the humility and courage to accept 100% responsibility for what he is responsible for.

What should he do if he realizes he has birthed or aggravated the conflict? He must humbly admit his sin in appropriate ways before God and others as needed. He must do whatever is necessary to clear his conscience.

Many, many times I have had to go to church members and say, "God has convicted me that what I did or said was wrong. Would you please forgive me?" The wise author of Proverbs said, "humility goes before honor" (Proverbs 18:12b). Most true believers are quickly willing to follow a pastor who they know has the integrity to admit his mistakes. They know he's not perfect, but they're waiting to see if he's honest and transparent.

It is always wise to take the high road in seeking to make sure there's nothing you have done that is wrong. I once discovered that a group of 25 men in the church I was pastoring had met secretly. They were led by a bitter, controlling man who was opposed to the direction of the church and who had specifically been asked by the leadership team not to convene the meeting. Regardless of that request, he had led them to meet and I was the main topic of discussion!

I thought, *"This was wrong and if these men are ever going to be right with God, they must make it right before God and others, including me."* In a few days, God brought the following passage to mind:

> *"If therefore you are presenting your offering at the altar, and there remember that your brother has something against you, leave your offering there before the altar, and go your way; first be reconciled to your brother, and then come and present your offering" (Matthew 5:23-24).*

I had always interpreted that passage to mean that if I had done something wrong to my brother and failed to repent and clear my conscience, then I shouldn't feign worship before God. This is true. But that's not all this passage means. It simply says, "If your brother has something against you." I realized that could be something legitimate (I had wronged him) or illegitimate (he just thinks I've wronged him but there's no real basis). God still commands me to go and seek reconciliation. Why? Because God is deeply committed to unity in the body. He wants every Christian to be proactive in seeking this unity, especially leaders.

So, I called each one of the men who had met secretly and then I met with them one-by-one.

"Apparently," I said, "I have done something that has offended you. I am committed to this church and to being the best leader I can be. Would you be honest with me in sharing what is bothering you? I commit to you that if God reveals to me any errors that I have made, or wrongs I have committed, I will be quick to admit my sin and change."

I discovered some areas where there were legitimate concerns, some that were misunderstandings and, (in this case), many that were totally false. But, there was not a man among them that could honestly accuse me of not seeking unity. Although I did not gain leadership capital with some of them, I did with many others as they observed this proactive response.

Leaders model. They should be an example of right behavior. And when they do something wrong they must model how to rectify wrong behavior. Appendix A contains a self-diagnosis tool entitled, *Fifty Marks of a Man of God.* These checkpoints are taken directly from 1 and 2 Timothy and Titus, letters written to young pastors. A few minutes spent before the Lord with this tool may help you see a problem in your own life and could save you days and perhaps months of difficulty if corrected. Don't instantly assume that you're not a part of the problem. The Bible gives many admonitions to pastors that would not be there if they were not needed (see 1 Timothy 3:1-7; I Peter 5:1-10; Titus 1:5-16; 2 Timothy 2:24-26; Acts 20:28-31).

If you have contributed to the problem, be humble and courageous enough to take responsibility and clear it up. Embrace this moment as an incredible opportunity for spiritual growth in your own life.

If you are reading this and are not the pastor, but you have a pastor with the serious issues previously described, you are in a dilemma. Several words of advice. First, the Bible tells us not to "accept an accusation against an elder except on the basis of two or three witnesses" (1 Timothy 5:19). There is a good reason for this. Pastors can get criticized a lot and are in the public eye. Be careful before you join in gossip that is unfounded. You must be extremely careful and factual before you "lift your hand against God's anointed" (1 Samuel 26:9). Moses' sister and brother faced consequences for that very step.

If it is evident that there is a serious problem with the pastor, a godly leader should do just as the Bible says and go to him and confront him in grace. (Matthew 18, Galatians 6). Do not talk to others, but to him directly. You may discover that what you're sensing is a misunderstanding or, if it is true, that your pastor is more than willing to adjust his life. Hopefully this will be the case.

If he fails to respond and the matter is genuinely serious it would be wise to get some counsel from the godliest counselor you know. This could be a pastor that you respect or trusted spiritual leader. There are those extreme times when it would be necessary to take one or two others with you to confront your pastor so that in the mouth of two or three others every fact may be confirmed and further confronted. What you CANNOT do is talk to others and mount a gossip campaign.

Pastors are not perfect and there have been hirelings in God's work. At times there may be the sad reality that church action must be taken to confront and deal with a sinning pastor who will not repent.

Sometimes it's the PEOPLE'S Fault

It just takes two people to have the tinder for the fire of conflict. People are relational (which is good) and sinful (which is bad). Believers, though eternally redeemed, are still strapped in this life with minds that are not fully renewed, emotions that are not fully tamed, and wills that are not completely surrendered. Great fuel for conflict.

The family of God is His tool for the advancement of His kingdom. As such, it instantly becomes Satan's primary target. If he can find or plant church members who can be tempted to sinful responses, he can destroy unity, impede progress, and foster misdirection. It makes sense that he would choose such a tactic. See Paul's warning about this to pastors in 1 Peter 5:1-10.

What are the potential problems in church members that can contribute to conflict?

Personal Sin. Sin always affects others and brings difficulty to the body of Christ. If none of us sinned, we'd have no conflict with each other at all! Paul wrote the entire book of 1 Corinthians to help sinning Christians resolve problems in the church. This church was not very far removed from the glories of the first church described in Acts 2 and yet they were already seeing the effects of human frailty on congregational life. In fact, such sinfulness erupted in the first few days of the early church (see Acts 5:1 and following).

Lost Church members. Christ told us this would happen. In fact, it is one of the main ploys of the enemy to "sow tares among the wheat" (Matthew 13:24-30). Unbelieving church members do not have the Spirit of God in them. Therefore, they are spiritually incapable of having the same values, same passion, and same power that true believers exhibit. If a man or woman has never genuinely submitted to the Lordship of Christ, they are still the lord of their life. They are in charge. When directions are taken that are uncomfortable to them they will react.

One of the evidences of this dilemma in the church is to see Christ's instructions for dealing with a sinning member. When church discipline reaches its final step and a so-called Christian has not repented you are to "treat him like an unbeliever" because at this point they are giving every indication of this fact (Matthew 18:17).

Confusion between principles and methods. Everyone has their preferences. There is nothing wrong with traditions. In fact, many traditions are helpful and effective. But it is easy to confuse a personal preference such as a certain style of music with a biblical principle. Principles never change, but church members and leaders alike should always hold methods with a loose hand.

Lack of burden for the world. Our innate self-centeredness is a constant pull away from our primary calling. The cancer of selfishness aborts evangelism. Many churches have been so inwardly focused for years that a call to a lifestyle that reaches others is a price they are unwilling to pay. When a pastor confronts this spiritual disease it often ignites reactions from selfish people.

Control. Without question, this is the primary issue that creates conflict in the church. A lost or self-centered church member who has never genuinely allowed Christ to have control over their life will never bend to anyone else's leadership. Brooks Faulkner, who was with the Southern Baptist Convention's LeaderCare division said national research from the 1980s and 1990s revealed that the leading cause of pastor fallout was "the control and power factor. 'Who's in charge' was one that kept surfacing," said Faulkner, who has 35 years experience counseling embittered pastors. "The second leading cause was lack of unity in the congregation. There's a small, but powerful minority of members, and there are factions in the congregation. Both have to do with who's in charge."

In the midst of my first great leadership challenge I was overwhelmed and confused. I was in an all-out battle for the soul of a church. We were really deciding who would be the final authority: God and what His word said or "the way we've always done it." My only solace was God and His word and I needed a huge daily dose to maintain enough perspective to put one foot in front of the other.

In the middle of my normal morning devotional time as I was reading Matthew 21, the Lord began to open my eyes to the real problem we were facing. In verse 23 the Pharisees (always the problem) asked a very revealing question of Christ: "By what authority are You doing these things, and who gave You this authority?" The issue with these men was authority. They wanted to be in control and Christ threatened this.

In the following verses Christ told two parables. One, of the father who had two sons and asked both of them to go work in the fields. One son said he would and didn't; another said he wouldn't and did. The next parable is about the vineyard owner who sent his servants and ultimately his son to collect his rightful proceeds from the vine growers. Apparently these self-centered workers thought they owned the farm, because they beat the servants and killed the son.

The connection between these stories is insightful. Many church members will say all day that they are willing to serve the Lord. But when you look for them in the fields (at a prayer meeting, a genuine time of worship, an evangelistic thrust) they are amazingly absent. Business meetings are never missed, but God meetings are avoided. When these moments occur, look up and you'll find the Pharisees have left the building. Generally, they have banded together outside and trumped up some silly reason to marginalize or disrupt those who are leading. They may couch this in spiritual words (*"I don't know what it is, but the pastor is just not feeding us anymore"* or, *"we've never really done it this way"* or, *"all he does is just preach about reaching the lost—what about us?"*). Don't be fooled. It is often nothing less than a deadly play for continued control. Their real statement, heard loudly by Christ and discerning leaders is, "I AM LOSING CONTROL AND I WON'T STAND FOR IT!"

And if you press them too hard they may kill you. In the middle of this particularly tough church battle I actually had a death threat. A deacon's wife wrote my wife a letter saying she was, "praying that your children will die of AIDS" (a direct quote). Unsurrendered church folks can be vicious when their control is threatened.

If you fail to understand this you will find yourself thinking things like, *"they're just really good people, maybe the change we're asking for is not right."* You may even take backward steps away from God's clear directives in His word. Evaluating the control element in your church is very, very important. Because only a right diagnosis can lead to right treatment. And only a right treatment can lead to a cure.

I've seen a lot of pastors and Christian leaders deeply wounded by Pharisees. I'm not justifying stupid decisions or impure motivations by pastors (we have our share of sins), but I have witnessed the assassination of too many good, godly pastors. How many churches have been choked to death by the unwillingness of a few strong opposing leaders? How much kingdom work has been strangled by their legalism? How many people have never heard the gospel because a church's voice was stifled by some dead, controlling church members? How many God-initiated plans have been thwarted by the strong hand of Pharisaical domination? You can see why Jesus spoke so loudly and often about this danger. He knew we needed to understand what was really happening and the church-killing danger of deferring to a Pharisee.

Jesus wouldn't put up with it. He confronted them, exposed them before His disciples, and refused to yield to their control. No fear of man would stop Him from doing His Father's will. He never sought peace at any price with these men. If God told him to eat with tax gatherers and sinners, redeem prostitutes, and heal men on the Sabbath, He relentlessly obeyed with no thought of the consequences. But to bend to a Pharisee was never in the equation.

Godly men must do the same. It will cause confrontation because you are never more dangerous to a Pharisee than when you challenge his authority. But you must not surrender control to unsurrendered men. Do not confuse the issue. *"They're not going to like this and it will cause trouble,"* never affected Christ. The trouble caused by bending to Pharisees and suffocating kingdom work is a fate worse than Pharisaical conflict. If you defer to them, they are leading the church whether you realize it or not.

It may cost you personally. You may be crucified, but like Christ, you will rise. In fact, Jesus' prediction about Pharisees in the last words of this chapter always comes true:

> *"Therefore I say to you, the kingdom of God will be taken away from you and given to a people, producing the fruit of it. And he who falls on this stone will be broken to pieces; but on whomever it falls, it will scatter him like dust" (Matthew 21:43-44).*

True fruit-producing followers of Christ, made so by their voluntary surrender to Christ's control, will inherit the kingdom. In the end, they will receive opportunity and authority, for their Father trusts them to lead under His direction. Controllers will always be broken beyond remedy. Like dead trees, their limbs are rigid and fragile, hollow and fruitless. They will degenerate into dust. A tragic end to an unbended life.

What's going on in your church? It's critical to put the

stethoscope to the church's heart and discover what's really happening. Our hurt or sinfulness or inexperience can blind us to the real problems...and misdiagnosis can be fatal.

It is often extremely valuable to get a second opinion by other trusted spiritual physicians. There are many older pastors who can give fantastic counsel. There are even men who specialize in this type of consultation. But, whatever you do, you are responsible before God to make a proper assessment.

It's a testimony to the power of God and the sovereignty of His plan that any church is healthy! But this is our greatest hope. We may struggle with our sinfulness, other's sinfulness, and the devil's attacks, but remember who is also working. God is more interested in the life of His Body than anyone else. It's His church, not ours. He is committed to its growth and has the resources to see that it succeeds. In fact, He's promised that "the gates of hell" will not prevail against this heaven-bound community. And remember this: it is a noble thing to give your life to build His church. Conflict is a part of the path to health.

NAVIGATION GATE #1:

- Take a few minutes to work through Appendix A prayer fully. Use a pen and mark every area that is an issue in your life. Then, faithfully seek to make spiritual adjust ments. It may help to share this with a godly mentor or friend that could help you see and be accountable to work on the weak areas in your life.

- Make a list, with trusted leaders if possible, of each issue that is a source of conflict in the church you serve. Let them read this chapter with you and begin to make a proper diagnosis of the church.

From: Matt Johnson
To: Jim Bradford
CC:
Subject: Will it make a difference?

Dear Jim,

I'm so sorry for bothering you again. But I have this nagging question that is really keeping me up at night. Honestly, if I can't get this settled I could see it driving me away from my current position. The question is this: if I go through this and take my family through what could be very difficult days, is it going to matter? This church has been straddling the fence for a long time. Is what I'm doing going to make a difference?

I know you're not God and can't answer this, but if I'm honest with myself I'd have to say I'm questioning the purpose of enduring conflict if there is no progress on the other side. Does that make sense?

Thanks for your time,

Matt

- -

From: Jim Bradford
To: Matt Johnson
CC:
Subject: RE: Will it make a difference

Dear Matt,

Every pastor wants to invest in what matters. The fact that you want your life to count, Matt, is not a wrong motivation. In fact, if you didn't have that desire I'd be really worried about you!

The reality is this: almost everything of value comes through conflict. It's not the impediment to progress, it's the doorway. You may not see all the benefits of the struggle this side of heaven, but if you'll handle this properly it will yield significant fruit. It mattered to Abraham, Moses, David, and most of all, Christ. Their willingness to face conflict and even death birthed life for themselves and those around them.

I believe in you and in a cause worth dying for,

Jim

CHAPTER TWO

FINDING PURPOSE

"Will it really matter?"

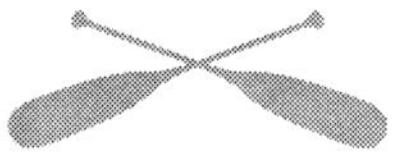

Rick Warren's book, *The Purpose-Driven Life,* has sold more copies than any non-fiction book in history other than the Bible, 35 million copies and counting. One of the most interesting things is that a disproportionate number of men bought this book—far more than usual. Warren hit the foundational nerve for men and women. Everyone wants to find and fulfill their purpose in life.

Pastors and church leaders are generally more interested in purpose than others. They understand something of eternity and the brevity of life. They realize what matters. They've given their lives to what they believe is a high calling. So when they find themselves in a situation that threatens to abort that purpose it's particularly troubling. And nothing seems more trivial or useless than church conflict. It always feels like sideways energy.

But to minimize the value of conflict is to be unaware of God's ways and human history. Change and progress always comes through conflict. Scan the biblical horizon. What do Abraham, Joseph, Moses, David, and Paul all have in common? They all went through conflict. In fact, we know them in large part because of the stories of their difficulties. Abraham and his enemies, Joseph and his brothers, Moses and the Egyptians plus three million grumbling Hebrews. David had his Saul, and Paul faced opposition in almost every city. It led to him being stoned, beaten, slandered, and imprisoned, but it also opened great doors for the gospel. The whole Bible is a story of conflict and resolution.

Look across church history. Luther, John Knox, Wilberforce, the list could go on and on. But the greatest conflict occurred with the greatest man. The Cross was all about conflict. The entire human race sent Christ to

Calvary. If He had not chosen at every turn to embrace conflict we would be lost forever. Conflict happens and conflict matters.

I have had seasons of prolonged conflict in two of the churches I've pastored over the last 40+ years. Both of those ultimately led to incredibly redemptive conclusions, but in the midst of those days I couldn't see it. In retrospect I wouldn't choose these moments, but I wouldn't trade them for anything. The privilege of writing this book and hopefully helping a few men of God along the way has come because of those battles. Conflict is filled with significance and should be seen for what it really is.

Conflict builds character. The average stay for a pastor in most churches in America now stands at 2-4 years. This is tragic. The honeymoon begins and things look great—conflict enters and the pastor leaves. One of the tragedies of these short tenures is that essential qualities and depth that can only be developed in the fires of conflict are never realized in a pastor's character.

The battles that I faced taught me more about myself and God than any other aspect of my ministry. It was there I learned of the sufficiency of God's grace, the faithfulness of His Word, the reality of man's sinfulness, the value of courage. Conflict was where I had to face and deal with my pride and man-fearing spirit that was more prominent than I ever would have realized. And one of the greatest lessons of my life—how to forgive—was stamped into my soul through those difficult days. I hate to think what I would be missing in my character if it were not for those life-changing seasons!

It is through conflict that the controlling elements that have brought stagnation and death to churches are exposed and conquered. One of the residual effects of pastors leaving at the first sight of conflict in a church is that this strengthens the hand of those who are in control. They gain more authority and power in the church. Run through a string of pastors over a few decades and you have a church that is firmly entrenched in its resistance. Only when the power brokers of a church are confronted by a courageous leader who will not bend and will not leave, are they exposed and change becomes a possibility.

Conflict is a great teacher to those around you. Even if the desired change does not occur in a church, it can happen in the lives of many. How valuable is it to see a man of God face difficulty with grace and truth? In that moment a man's courage and character are teaching and developing many in his flock. Courage inspires courage: "*If he can go through that, I suppose I can face my difficulties.*" A willingness to embrace conflict for a great cause and then a proper, godly handling of all the components of that conflict speaks volumes. It may be your greatest sermon.

But the most important reason for embracing conflict is that it matters to God. He is the sole judge of all that happens. He has eternal purposes we know nothing about. He is the One who gives the final accounting. And He matters.

By the grace of God I think I can honestly say that I don't think I ever went to a pastorate unless God called me. And I believe that He took me to each field on purpose. I was to faithfully shepherd and lead that flock, regardless of its condition, to the best of my ability. He had the right to place me wherever He desired. In spite of my weaknesses, He thought I should be there for my sake, their sake, or both. Therefore, I never felt the freedom to leave unless He told me to go. A church didn't determine my calling, God did. Conflict was just a part of the job and often was an indicator that I was doing my job. I never intended to stir up controversy (who in the world is that dumb?) but if it came as a result of God-initiated plans, then I believe it was a necessary season. I didn't see this at first, but time has made this very clear.

Please understand that I'm not saying that I did everything right by a long shot. I'm sure I've created plenty of unnecessary conflict along the way. But if I did, it was never intentional.

Has God called you to your church? If so, you are their shepherd. Sheep can be messy, wayward, stubborn. Everything you see in your life in your worst moments, any church member is capable of…and more. We are called to lead them in the midst of their sin and need. If our tenure was determined by the church's responses, most pastors would quit every Monday! God has called you to take your church family through seasons of joy and productivity, sadness and conflict…by God's grace, to do the best you can to lead them to Him.

My brother, Tom, served for a season as missionary in Africa. He once drove many hours into the bush with a crusty old missionary to visit a tribe that, to their knowledge, had never heard the gospel. It was a horrible trip over a rough road for eight hours. They faced such great opposition on the ride that my brother began to think it was going to be a tremendously productive ministry in light of the enemy's attack.

When they got to the tribe they set up a projector to show a film about Christ. Not only did the people laugh and scoff at them, but not one single person responded to their invitations to follow Christ. And then my brother realized they had another long trip home!

They drove along in silence for many miles. Finally the old missionary asked Tom if he was disappointed that they didn't see anyone come to Christ.

"Absolutely," my brother replied.

"Do you know why I've been on the mission field all these years?" the old missionary asked.

"I assumed it's to lead people to Christ," Tom replied.

"No, that's not why I'm here," he said to Tom's amazement.

"Oh, don't get me wrong. I live my life to see people come to Christ. But I am here because Jesus told me to come. I may be a planter, or a cultivator, or a harvester. I may be here so that these people have a chance to hear the gospel and won't be able to stand in the judgment and accuse God of not giving them an opportunity. The results are not my business. I'm here because Christ told me to come. I am simply serving Him."

In the final analysis, church leaders serve an audience of ONE. "It is the Lord Christ whom we serve," Paul said. "We make it our ambition…to please Him" (2 Corinthians 5:9).

As you are tossed by the whitewater of church conflict, are you still in love with Him? Are you still in love with His Bride? Are you loving your people as "Christ loved the church and gave Himself for her?" Are you faithfully being "on guard for yourself and your flock, over which the Holy Spirit has made you overseers" (Acts 20:28)?

It may not make sense to others, even to you at times, but it matters greatly to God.

Navigation Gate #2:

- Keep a running list in your journal of everything good that God is doing through this experience, in you, your family, and your church. Meditate on this list regularly and give thanks. This gratitude may seem trivial but it could maintain your perspective and help you remain faithful until death.

From: Matt Johnson
To: Jim Bradford
CC:
Subject: drowning

Dear Jim,

I've spent some time with our leadership team and some other buddies and I think I'm getting a fairly good assessment of what's going on in our church. Thanks so much for your counsel to stop and make a proper diagnosis.

But I don't know if I'm going to make it. I feel like I'm going under. There are nights where I just can't turn off my mind. The "what if" wheel starts spinning. I could see this thing exploding and I'm right at the epicenter.

Even if I can find the right path to lead the church forward, I'm not sure I've got the emotional resources to see it through.

Forgive me for babbling, but inside, I'm screaming, or crying, or…I don't know what.

Help!

Matt

- -

From: Jim Bradford
To: Matt Johnson
CC:
Subject: RE: drowning

Dear Matt,

Have you considered selling shoes yet? I got there once! I thought, "anything is better than this," and it took a while for some folks to talk me off the ledge!

I want to say perhaps the most important thing I could ever tell you. You're not going to survive this without God. If you try to handle this emotionally, with mere human resources, you'll blow a fuse.

Surprisingly, in retrospect, I see now that the conflicts I endured led me to phenomenal places I couldn't discover any other way. I found Him. Intimacy is the key, Matt, and if you don't find God and find Him deeply in the midst of this, you'll be a statistic. I've taken the liberty to enclose a few notes that might help you, but please hear this: find HIM. He's there and He's not silent.

Praying with you,

Jim

CHAPTER THREE

Maintaining Intimacy

"How can I survive?"

Every conflict you ever face is ultimately about you and God. It may not start there, but God has planned for it to go there. Our Father is dramatically interested in raising sons and daughters who know Him. Therefore, he sometimes orchestrates and always oversees events that bring us to the end of ourselves. These flash points are often excruciating and in our pain we will make one of four decisions:

1. *Will I just gut it out?*

2. *Will I run away?*

3. *Will I compromise?*

4. *Will I find God here?*

Those who choose the latter discover an intimacy that is never found in less stressful seasons. When we're desperate and searching, God becomes very real.

Intimacy with God provides certain things during conflict that cannot be found anywhere else, and it's essential for your survival.

Perspective. We lose sight of reality in times of conflict. Clouded by the hurt in our soul, the betrayal of people we thought we could trust, and the fog of conflicting ideas, we can't see well.

The Psalmist recorded his confusion (Psalm 73). When things weren't going well for him and his enemies seemed to prosper, he got very upset and asked, "Why have I kept my hands pure?" He became like a senseless beast in his thinking "until," he said, "I came into the sanctuary of my God. Then I perceived their end." He saw the truth and the end conclusion was "the nearness of God is my good." Such life altering insight can be found in only one place...God's presence.

There is no one (and I mean no one) who sees your conflict like God. He knows who's right and who's wrong. He sees what's next and what your options are. He knows where He's taking things and why it's all happening. He is aware of who is His friend and who's not. He has perspective and He is anxious to give this to all who will take the time to wait in His presence.

Everyone is capable of making terrible knee-jerk decisions without this view. It's only gained through time with Him.

Direction. Christ is the Head of His church and He knows what He's doing! He knows when people need to be confronted or comforted. He is very clear about what battles should be fought and the best tactical methods. He is the ultimate Leader and understands leadership principles better than any self-professed leadership guru. He describes Himself as "the Way" (John 14:6) and is anxious to "lead (us) in the right paths for His Name's sake" (Psalm 23).

How do you think you could possibly lead without listening to Him? If you will take the necessary time in His presence, you can move at His initiation and He has the opportunity to literally lead His church through you. But if you do not maintain intimacy with Him during times of conflict you must generate the directions yourself. And you're not that good!

Development. God is out to build men and women for eternity. C.S.Lewis, speaking of the future state of glorified saints said that those who know Christ are potential "gods and goddesses...there are no ordinary people. You have never met a mere mortal" (*Weight of Glory*, C.S. Lewis).

In this life God is conforming us to the image of His Son and preparing us to rule and reign with Him in eternity. Every good leader became such through the crucible of conflict and testing. This training is not only about now, but eternity.

These moments are essential to our development. Only in His presence do we begin to understand this. Only there do we take a breath long enough to hear what He is working on in our lives. Those who fail to listen and rush forward may abort His purposes and stunt their growth. Those who meet with God grow at a healthy pace. Each conflict, properly navigated, builds them up into the "measure of the stature of the fullness of Christ" (Ephesians 4:12-13).

Grace. Grace is that supernatural quality of God which gives us what we need. "I can't handle this," Paul cried out three times. The Lord promised He was going to give sufficient grace—and He did. It was so strengthening that Paul came to the point where he would literally "glory" in his weaknesses. He knew the weaker he was, the more he would experience God's supernatural empowering (2 Corinthians 12:7-10).

Grace is found in God's presence. He gives grace to the humble. A proud man who runs around in conflict barking orders, manipulating the process, or frantically putting duct tape on the hole in the Titanic receives nothing from God. Humility is seen in a man who takes time to get in the Lord's presence, cry out to Him in prayer, and listen to Him through His Word.

Your level of pride can be easily determined by how little you pray. If you think you can go a day, week, or month without praying or spending time in His Word, it's clear evidence you proudly believe you can live your life without God. The humble spend time with Him. The humble get grace and there is no season in which you need it more than in conflict.

Peace. There is no substitute for this. Conflict is war. His presence is like a fortress and "the righteous run into it and are safe" (Proverbs 18:10). When we are praying and trusting in genuine daily, hourly communion with Him His peace mounts guard like a sentry over our hearts (Philippians 4:7).

In fact, this is one of the greatest testimonies to those who are observing us under this stress. Such peace encourages our supporters and is tremendously disconcerting and convicting to our enemies.

Promises. God makes promises. Lots of them. In fact, He wrote down over 7,000 of them in His word just for us. A biblical promise births faith in our hearts and gives us the confidence to face things that don't make sense. It also binds our heart to His in greater affection. It is times of difficulty that drive us to read His word and rely on Him through His promises. Peter assured us that these "exceeding great and precious promises," combined with His enabling power within us, would give us everything we need for "life and godliness" (2 Peter 1:1-4).

In the midst of my worst church conflict a very bitter man was opposing me and the directions the Lord had given us. He was pushing for a showdown and despite all our best efforts it was inevitable. The night before what turned about to be a five-hour business meeting (I'd never allow that now, but I was young and pretty doggone stupid!) the Lord told me to be quiet and let Him defend me. He gave me these promises:

> *"He has dug a pit…and will fall into the hole which he made" (Psalms 7:15).*
>
> *"The Lord will fight for you as you keep silent" (Exodus 14:14).*
>
> *"An evil man is ensnared by the transgression of his lips, but the righteous will escape from trouble" (Proverbs 12:13).*

I climbed up on top of those promises and sat down and was able to walk into that excruciating meeting with clear direction and absolute peace. True to His word, it all transpired exactly as God had promised. It was miraculous. My detractor had planned a "pit" for me, which he ended up falling into. I merely kept silent and the men of our church stood up in biblical defense. And his own lips and the lips of his family members uttered the most incriminating statements made that evening. I know from experience that you can trust the promises of the God of the universe. And He has some with your name on them hidden in His secret place.

Finding God

So how do I access God's presence? When we're in crisis, sometimes the last thing we feel like doing is spending time with God! The following will give us some practical suggestions that have been hammered out on the anvil of my own experiences.

Find Him before the conflict. A study was done more than 15 years ago that found that the average American pastor spends only seven minutes a day in devotional reading and prayer! Living in God's presence is an art that is cultivated through many years. This is why the Psalmist encouraged us to "seek the Lord while He may be found…surely in a flood of great waters you shall not find Him" (Psalm 32:6).

God is always willing to be found, but our spiritual abilities may be weak if they have not been developed through seasoned practice.

Get up! If you can't sleep, or if the Lord wakes you up early, get up. He has something to say that you need. He is waiting to equip you with what He knows is essential for the day. My best times are these early moments. Through the years I've learned (for the most part!) to cooperate with Him in this. If it's 3 a.m. and He's calling, get up. Read and pray until He takes you back to sleep or into the day.

You can catch up later and I promise you what He has to say is more important than a few hours of sleep. Many men have lived in worry, fear, and misdirection simply because they would not get out of bed to hear God. A wise man said, "A little sleep, a little slumber, a little folding of the hands to rest and your poverty will come in like a vagabond and your need like an armed man" (Proverbs 6:10-11).

I always wonder what I will miss and really need later if I fail to cooperate with God's schedule. Conversely, you will find yourself amazingly refreshed physically if you get into God's presence.

Read! There is absolutely no substitute for the simple reading of God's word. During times of conflict I read in my normal pattern, but I may add a heavy dose of Psalms and Proverbs. Psalms gives me perspective from men who've been there, Proverbs—wisdom. Both are critical. As you read, listen for His voice. We're not out to run through a reading, but to encounter HIM.

J.C. MacCauley said, "I read Thy word, O Lord, each passing day and in Thy sacred page find glad employ. But this I pray: save from the killing letter. Teach my heart—set free from human forms—the holy art of reading Thee in every line, in precept, prophecy, and sign. Till all my vision filled with Thee Thy likeness shall reflect in me. Not knowledge, but Thyself my joy! For this I pray."

It's about encountering Him.

Record! Something amazing happens to us when we journal what God is saying to us. Not only is there a very practical benefit of dramatically increased retention, but thoughts become, "unentangled when they go through the lips and over the fingertips." When we think through something enough to write it down, the truth is digested and becomes ours. It feeds us in new, nourishing ways.

Recording what God is saying—even if it's a few lines or a paragraph—gives us the ability to go back and find these nuggets when we need them. It also gives us the capacity to share them with others. In the worst conflict I ever endured in a church I had pages and pages of things God said to me. They carried me. And because I had written them down, I had ready access to these truths for future use.

My family has a journal of my grandfather's experiences with God. What a blessing it is to read of God's faithful provision and my granddad's faith! I am challenged by them and so grateful he took the time to record his times with God. I hope my grandchildren will one day say the same.

Remain! God's desire is not for us to spend an hour or so with Him, but to abide in His presence. To abide means to, "remain in a stable or fixed position." Jesus reminds us, recorded so beautifully in John 15, that we can produce nothing without this constant abiding in the Vine.

Paul told us to "pray without ceasing" (1 Thessalonians 5:17). I once thought this was impossible, but realized God cannot ask us to do anything we can't do with the aid of His grace. It is possible and mandatory for those who want to experience Him. Prayer is the air we breathe, the atmosphere we are to live in. God is so gracious that He surrounds us with multiple pressures so we will recognize our need without ceasing…and come to Him. Conflict is an incredible opportunity to learn to abide.

Share! Tell others what God is showing you. It will drive this truth deeper down into your soul—encouraging them and developing you. And when the leaders around you hear that God is speaking to you it will dramatically increase their confidence in you as a leader as well as their faith in God. God is speaking to you in the quiet hours not only for your sake, but for theirs. In times of conflict everyone is shaky. People look to a leader to have a word from God…and they should.

Hear Him through godly friendships. Many years ago a pastor that I admired beyond all others fell morally. I realized that if he could fall, I could fall. I needed the deep accountability of trusted friends. I called three dear pastor buddies to join me in an accountability retreat to ask each other the hard questions. As of this writing, that retreat has continued annually for 16 years. And it has turned into much more. This band of brothers has carried me, encouraged me, challenged me, and corrected me more times than I can count. They have been used by God to speak His truth into me—particularly in seasons of conflict. We talk now on a weekly basis.

Every pastor needs this in his life but it doesn't happen overnight and must be aggressively pursued. Godly colleagues can be a strong channel for the voice of God to your soul and an invaluable source for your survival during difficult days.

Pray with others! Just as you need time in God's presence, so do others in your church. It may be that God is waiting for you to become desperate enough to cry out corporately to Him in prayer—not only for your own survival, but for the furtherance of His kingdom through His Body.

In a time of great crisis, I finally realized there was nothing I could humanly do to bring change. We needed God. I called the church to 40 days of fasting and prayer and told them I would be at the church every morning of the week at 6:30 a.m. for an hour of intercession. About 30-40 people joined me. At the end of those six weeks, God had so clearly manifested Himself in our presence that we decided to continue. That prayer meeting lasted for 18 months, every day of the workweek. I don't know if I have ever, or will ever again, experience the depth of that prayer experience. I wouldn't trade anything for it and for all we experienced together in God's presence. Much was accomplished for God's glory through the prayers of those faithful intercessors. The church I now pastor was birthed out of that prayer meeting and has been the greatest and healthiest ministry experience of my life.

Of all the amazing things about God, the most startling to me is that God wants to be known. Accessibility is His most remarkable attribute. That the God of the Universe would condescend to human understanding is mind boggling. David said to his son Solomon, "As for you, my son Solomon, know the God of your father…if you seek Him, He will let you find Him" (1 Chronicles 28:9).

He backs up His desire by aggressive self-disclosure. Never waiting for us, He displays Himself in every cloud, shouts from every mountain, and blows in fall breezes and spring tornados. "Day by day" His creation "brings forth speech" (Psalm 19:2).

He's gone to extraordinary lengths to give black-and-white revelation. His Word unveils His character with every stroke of the pen, just as your word reveals you. He can be known through the Bible. In fact, that's the point—over 1,000 pages that say, "Here I am."

If that were not enough, He laid aside all of His rights and privileges as God and poured Himself into human flesh. "The Word of God dwelt among us and we beheld His glory" (John 1:14).

God was saying, "Do you want to know Me? What I think, how I act, what I value, what I invest in, what matters? Then look at Me," and there He was in human flesh. As He sat with children we viewed His compassion, by Peter His stability, by Mary Magdalene His grace, with the Pharisees His courage. A fuller picture has never been painted. "If you've seen Me, you've seen the Father" (John 14:9).

And His Spirit helps us in our weakness. How could we ever view God through filthy lenses smudged by sin? So He blows through our minds with the purifying wind of His Spirit and the washing of the water of the Word, enlightening, convicting, communicating. "Things which eye has not seen, nor ear heard, nor which have ever even entered the heart of man...God reveals them through His Spirit" (1 Corinthians 2:9-11).

What amazing help He gives so we may know Him! And some of the times He shouts the loudest are during the excruciating moments of conflict.

For all of this He asks one thing: "Seek Me. Lay aside other vain affections (they'll produce nothing of value) and make the main occupation of your life the pursuit of the Holy." We need this constant call, for our heads are easily turned by Satan's sequined substitutes: the worries of the world, the tyranny of the urgent, the demons of fear, the loud voices of the crowd. To find Him takes time and attention, not because He's hiding, but because our deceived minds are only slowly convinced of His value.

Those who know Him—really know Him—are the joyful few who give themselves wholly to the task, who pay the price for intimacy with the Almighty. Why would we ever look elsewhere?

Navigation gate #3:

- Set a date for a weekly or monthly all-day spiritual retreat to spend concentrated time in reading God's Word and prayer. Make it a priority to continue these retreats indefinitely, realizing that the Enemy will do everything in his power to try to abort your time with God.
- Consider an extended fast to lay aside the constant roar of other voices so you may hear Him more clearly. There is a dynamic power in this discipline when approached spiritually. It may be that the answers and anointing you need are waiting for you through such a time with Him.

From: Matt Johnson
To: Jim Bradford
CC:
Subject: thanks

Dear Jim,

I just wanted to drop you a note and let you know how grateful I am for your input into my life. I know you're busy and your time is valuable, but the relationship we're developing is an incredible blessing to me.

I've got a lot to learn and I guess I never realized how important other men were in my life to help me. Particularly in this time of conflict I feel like I would be overwhelmed if I didn't have someone to talk to whose counsel I respect. Thanks for being such a gracious mentor!

Grateful,

Matt

- -

From: Jim Bradford
To: Matt Johnson
CC:
Subject: RE: thanks

Dear Matt,

Well, it's mutual. I've never connected with another man that it didn't help me more than it helped him!

On that note, I think there's a further step you might consider. Everybody, and particularly every pastor, needs two vital relationships in his life that are often missing: close friendships and strategic mentors. I'm thrilled that you would think of me as a mentor, Matt, and I have a real joy in fulfilling some of that role. But I want to ask you another question: do you have some close friends? Two or three guys that you can be transparently honest with and they'd still be there for you?

Life is too short to not develop friendships, Matt, and I sense that you might need what I'm enclosing. Read it carefully and pursue it aggressively. I think you'll unearth a gold mine.

Your friend,

Jim

CHAPTER FOUR

Gaining Counsel

Is there any help?

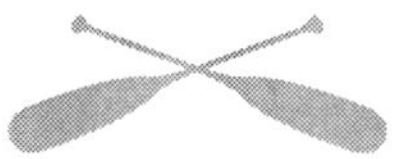

Several years ago my three pastor friends and I were walking through a hotel lobby together, laughing and enjoying the fruits of a long-built relationship. We noticed an older pastor that we deeply admired sitting alone at a table. He was a man had developed one of the greatest churches in America and who had counseled each of us individually at times. He called us to come join him. After a few minutes of light conversation he looked at the four of us with a serious sadness in his eyes.

"I envy you guys," he said. "I see you every year at this convention and you are always together. I've watched you for years and your deep friendship is very noticeable. You know," he continued, "I spent all my life building my church and I never took time to build friendships with other pastors. Now it's to late. I've come to the point where I really need it, but honestly, I don't have a single close friend in the world."

I have never forgotten that moment. A recent study showed that 70% of the pastors in America say they do not have anyone they consider a close friend. Satan has done his job well. He has a devious strategy to isolate us. He works hard to keep us away from intimate relationships with others because he knows that such friendships are a powerful weapon against his agenda.

When difficulties and conflict come, our isolation becomes even more acute. We feel it more deeply. "I alone, oh Lord, am left as a prophet in Israel," we cry as we find ourselves depressed under a tree like Elijah. The lack of friends can lead to depression, self-pity, and ultimately a hopelessness that devastates us. Sadly, it could have been avoided.

Friendship barriers

Air is readily available. We breathe it in everyday. We hardly ever notice it's presence, but it is essential for health. Friends to whom we can turn for godly counsel and support are just as important. Without them our emotional lungs are malnourished. So what is it that keeps us from inhaling these lifesaving relationships?

Busyness. Developing these kinds of friendships takes time. Most pastors are consumed with the tyranny of the urgent and don't stop to develop deep relationships. Many men would feel guilty if they took time out to play golf, retreat, or simply have coffee with another pastor on a regular basis.

Fear. Some of us are simply afraid. Fueled by all kinds of past experiences, we think openness and transparency will expose us in a way that's beyond our comfort level. And, if we have not died to our love of reputation, we seek to maintain a facade of perfection. We fail to realize that transparency makes people love us more. Every true follower of Christ is awed by a man who is open and honest about his life. They know the sins and failings of their own lives and a transparent friend with whom they can be honest is like a breath of fresh air on a spring morning.

Hurt. We may have been wounded by a familiar friend in the past. Consciously or unconsciously we are holding others at arm's length. It has become our strategy to avoid further pain. David, the shepherd king of Israel, had known such a wound. But his humility led him to see it for what it was, release it before the Lord, and continue to deepen relationships with men who would live and die for him. Don't let a past wound keep you from a present source of healing.

Lack of knowledge. Some have never experienced deep, collegial friendships simply because they didn't know how to accomplish it. If they knew better, they'd do better. "*How do I start? What is a legitimate amount of time to spend pursuing friendships for my soul's sake? Who can I trust? How aggressive should I be?*"

We may not know how to build friendships and we may not even know how to get good counsel in times of trouble or recognize it's importance, but if we're going to be healthy we need to push forward.

Pride. There's no easy way to say this, but often our failure here is nothing more than unvarnished pride. We think we can make it by ourselves. In our arrogance we assume we are better than other men and more capable. God is extremely committed to removing pride from His servants' hearts. It may even be that the purpose of the exercise in a current problem is to deal with this deadly virus. Isolation because of arrogance must be ruthlessly dealt with by recognition and repentance.

You need a friend

Why are friendships and godly counsel so important? Why should I give myself to this development?

We all need someone we can unload on who will love us in the end. This should never take the place of our relationship with our wife, but men need other men to successfully process life. In the movie, "First Knight," there is a line that has always impressed me. As a man is initiated into King Arthur's round table, he stands facing each knight individually with their hand on each other's shoulders and they both recite these words: "Face to face, brother to brother, one in life and death." Something stirs a man's soul when he hears words like this. When he knows that there will be a man by his side during the good times and bad.

The writer of Proverbs gives us another reason for building these friendships.

"For by wise counsel you will wage war and in abundance of counselors there is victory" (Proverbs 24:6).

You don't have all the answers. If you think you do, you're in more trouble than you realize. Godly counsel has always helped every plan I've developed. I work with a leadership team in my current church. I believe in the plurality of leadership. It provides a phenomenal safety for both our congregation and myself. But more than that, we're better together. It's not always easy, but it's always better when properly and biblically applied. God said there's victory there, and I just suppose He knows what He's talking about!

Further, no man can handle the full load of church leadership, particularly in times of conflict and difficulty. We need men around us who will hold up our arms. When we get battle weary these men will help us. And, when they are tired, we aid them. There is strength in these relationships that can be supplied no other way. I have been blessed with some deep friendships both inside and outside the church. It would be impossible to express how many times they have encouraged me challenged me and kept me going.

I once heard a man say that the last person to realize there is a tear in the back of his jacket is the one who's wearing it. Real friends can be used by God to help us see blind spots. This often happens as they share their own struggles and needs, and this helps you see the same issue in your own character. Real friends love each other enough to tell the truth and there is enough relational trust that this tough love can be accepted.

I would also add that there are different levels of relationships that are all important to our health. Friendships should be our first line of defense. There are also older mentors that are vital. These are men we look to for counsel and training. They may not become the one we go fishing with, but they fulfill a deep need in our development. These may be men we go to again and again or they may also be men we only connect with a few times. I have had a number of mentors like this in my spiritual and professional journey. With some I have had regular, ongoing conversations and they were aware of their mentoring function. Others have counseled me without even knowing the vital role they were playing.

Your next step

Friendships and the openness to receive counsel don't just happen. They must be built. How do we begin?

Pray. Do you think God knows what you need emotionally and relationally? Do you think He could help you? If so, it's time to pray. Ask God to give you the courage to reach out to someone. Pray that He will bring to your mind a potential friend—in fact, I would ask Him for THREE GOOD FRIENDS. Further, I would ask Him to bring into your life someone to be a mentor to you. You may discover that they are already there and the relationship just needs a little cultivation.

Initiate. You've got to start. Years ago I had the devastating experience of watching the man I trusted and admired the most fall morally. It crushed me. He was a godly man who had been greatly used of God. It took me awhile to recover from the shock. A wise, godly mentor in my life (Manley Beasley) told me, "Bill, this is no longer about him...it's about you. God wants to develop something in your life and you need to discover what it is." Many things came from that momentary exchange. But one of the most valuable was the recognition of my own vulnerability. If this godly man could fall, I could fall. I needed some men in my life that knew me well enough to ask me the hard questions and wouldn't give up on me if I gave the wrong answers. I needed close friends.

I called three pastor buddies that I had the closest relationship with and bared my soul. I asked them if they felt the same fear (which they did to varying degrees) and if they would go on an accountability retreat with me. It took some persistence and schedule wrangling, but one Sunday night we found ourselves in a little cabin together for a three-day retreat. I had prepared a simple self-evaluation sheet and we took the first night working through that privately. The next morning we began to share together what we had discovered. It was one of the most meaningful and powerful moments of our lives. We laughed and prayed and encouraged. After three days of sharing and praying (and a little golf and a lot of good food on the side!) we left vowing this would become an annual experience.

This past April was our 16th retreat. But it has become much more than that. We now talk to each other weekly and retreat more than once a year. We do study breaks together. We show up at each other's anniversaries. We celebrate and enjoy life together. Other than my relationship with my family, these friendships are the greatest relational treasure I have and are more valuable to me than any earthly possession.

Build friendships within your church. Many men have told me that this is impossible. I think that is ridiculously unbiblical. In every church I've pastored God has given my wife and me many cherished friendships and at least one couple that was a deep friendship. We currently have some friends that we travel with, play with, pray with, and enjoy life. The husband is a man that holds confidences. I can "goof off" with him or talk seriously about my life and struggles. Time with them is an oasis both for my wife and me. They have blessed us and loved us through many difficulties. It is an incredible treasure.

Develop friendships with area pastors. If you think about it, you would realize that there is really only one church in the city. God gives many local expressions of that body, but the church of the Lord Jesus Christ is composed of all those who truly know Him. In that light, there are a multitude of shepherds for this one flock. We ought to know each other. We should be connected through prayer and relationship for the development of the kingdom in our city. And, there are some strategic initiatives that can be realized from these friendships.

Many years ago a group of pastors in our city became deeply concerned for revival in our community. Our city had been highlighted as having the third highest murder rate in the nation. The mayor called on the church leaders for help. We didn't know what to do but we felt compelled to join together and pray. A few pastors met with a real heart burden and it grew. We began to pray together monthly. Later we discovered the Prayer Summit movement that began in the northwest and we invited some of those men to come help us in a three-day prayer summit. About 25 pastors, led by two facilitators, went to a retreat center one January with the goal of doing nothing but praying together.

The first morning was slow and stilted, but by mid-afternoon an amazing thing happened—*Jesus walked into the room*! The presence of the Lord graciously interrupted our pride and timidity. Men began being transparent. Confession flowed, forgiveness happened. Songs erupted spontaneously from our souls. After three days in God's presence, we were blood brothers. We developed a leadership team to help foster this movement in the city. We have continued that retreat every year and out of these relationships have come incredible spiritual movement. In a recent study, George Barna said that our city, Little Rock, Arkansas, had more people per capita attending church than any major city in America. I have no idea all the reasons for this, but I cannot help but believe that the relationship of these pastors is one of the factors in this kingdom growth.

We love each other, cheer for each other, and help each other. There are some of the pastors who, along the way, have developed deep personal friendships that have been invaluable. I will never forget the moment when one of the pastors' wives died. When he walked into her funeral, 25 pastors were standing together in the crowd to support him. Whether it's through your denominational relationships or cross-denominational, become a part of the lives of other pastors in the city. You need them and they need you!

God's initiative

Remember the old joke about the man in the flood who cried out to God for help. A neighbor came by in a boat and invited him to jump in but the brother replied, "God is going to rescue me." Later he had to retreat to the rooftop, still trusting in the Lord. A rescue helicopter hovered overhead and offered help, but he replied, "I'm trusting in the Lord." Finally the floodwaters overwhelmed him and took his life. Waking up in heaven he said with frustration, "Lord, why didn't you rescue me?" The Lord lovingly replied, "I sent a boat and a helicopter—what more did you want?"

You might be surprised. God may have friends and mentors all around you that He has strategically placed for your good and His glory. Help may be closer than you think.

NAVIGATION GATE #4:

- Pray, asking God to help you find three good friends. Perhaps a good start would be to ask a pastor buddy for coffee and share your heart. Don't give up even if he is tentative in his response. He may need it more than you!

- If you want to take a really bold step, call the three best friends you have and plan a retreat or outing with a strategic soul-development purpose in mind. Center your time together around 3-5 good questions. *What's going on in your life right now? How do you think God wants to use you in the next ten years? What is there in your life that might abort that potentially if not addressed and overcome?*

- Ask God further who is to be the next mentor in your life. Call him and make an appointment to share what is going on in your life and seek his counsel.

From: Matt Johnson
To: Jim Bradford
CC:
Subject: Where in the world do I start?

Dear Jim,

Thanks for the last emails. They helped…tremendously. I think I see now the value of fighting through these things and that my personal survival and leadership must be directed by time spent in God's presence. I also see that I really need some close friends to be God's voice to me during this time and beyond.

I guess one of the next things on my mind is this: where do I start? It seems that everywhere I look in our church there is something that needs to be addressed. In the current emotional climate any issue can explode into a major battle.

Got any thoughts, oh wise one?

Your young son in the faith,

Matt

- -

From: Jim Bradford
To: Matt Johnson
CC:
Subject: Where in the world do I start?

Dear Matt,

Easy on the "wise one" there, Matt! I'm just a fellow pilgrim, but I do suppose I've got a few more battle scars!

This is a tough one. What needs to be addressed in one church should be left alone in another at a different moment. There are, though, certain non-negotiables that a church must address or they will never move forward in their mission.

As always, God has given us the ability to know His Word, hear His Spirit, and utilize godly counselors to lead us. And there are certain practical steps to determine when some things should be addressed and how to address them. It will take longer than this email to explain, so I've enclosed a little more detailed discussion. Hope it helps.

Your fellow learner,

Jim

CHAPTER FIVE

Choosing Battles

"Where do I wade in?"

The Battle of New Orleans took place on January 8, 1815, and was the final major battle of the War of 1812. American forces, commanded by General Andrew Jackson, defeated an invading British Army intent on seizing New Orleans and the vast territory America had acquired with the Louisiana Purchase. The only problem was, *the war was already over*! The Treaty of Ghent had been signed on December 24,1814, but news of the peace would not reach the troops until February. It was a battle that didn't need to be fought.

God's timing is critical in dealing with change in the life of His church. There are many battles that we don't engage in that we should. There are some that we should never touch that we walk into with guns blazing! Discovering how to know the difference is one of the challenges of pastoral leadership.

The Non-negotiable of God-initiation

One of my mentors, Manley Beasley, told me once that, "the mark of a godly church is that everything they do is God-initiated." I love that statement which was modeled so clearly by Christ. Several times in the book of John, Christ describes his life this way.

> *So Jesus said, "When you lift up the Son of Man, then you will know that I am He, and I do nothing on My own initiative, but I speak these things as the Father taught Me. And He who*

> *sent Me is with Me; He has not left Me alone, for I always do the things that are pleasing to Him" (John 8:28-29).*
>
> *"For I did not speak on My own initiative, but the Father Himself who sent Me has given Me a commandment as to what to say and what to speak (John 12:49).*

This has always made pastoring easier for me, in one sense. My job is not to come up with new ideas, new things to say, new plans. My job is to stay so connected to the Spirit of God and His Word that I am hearing from Him. I am to say what He tells me to say, to push what He pushes, to do what He is doing, to go where He's going. Simple.

The harder question is discerning the difference between my voice, others' voices, and His. But if He tells me that I am to live and lead by His initiative, then there is a way to fulfill this. It takes some time and practice for any pastor to become a man who moves by God's leadership alone, but it can be done and must be done.

That's one of the reasons God says His church is to be led by a plurality of leaders. An Elder team or leadership team should be a group of godly men who are charged with the task of together hearing the voice of God. The Senior Pastor on that team, with the particular gifting and calling God has placed on him, should be looked to most often for directional leadership. But it is others' responsibility to think and pray and counsel together with him so that they affirm and further discover the will of God for the church. "In abundance of counselors is victory" (Proverbs 24:6), is not a casual suggestion for leaders but the pathway to clarity about God's initiation. Further, the counsel of other godly Christian leaders and friends outside the church can be invaluable in times of conflict or change.

Thankfully, God has given an objective and comprehensive record of what He wants us to do. It's called the Bible. Our job is to "rightly divide" the Word—to cut it straight with no deviation. I had a seminary professor who often said, "When the Bible says a lot about something, you say a lot; when it says little, you say little." We are to major on what the Word majors on.

Our goal as a pastor is not to start with a problem and attack, but to start with God's Word and cast His vision. As you do this, you may find yourself encountering barriers to that vision that must naturally be addressed, but it is done in light of what God has said and is initiating, not as an isolated battle.

When do we move forward? When God speaks!

The Value of Comprehensive Planning

Along with this, genuine pastors are men who know their flock. Shepherds in Jesus' day watched the condition of their herds. They knew where the food and water was and what they needed to accomplish each day. They had a plan for those sheep each year. One of the major components of our calling as pastors and elders is to "oversee," which means to look at and understand the big picture and lead our people there. Sadly, many pastors have received very little training or modeling in this area.

Not only should we know our flock (our local church) we should become great students of our potential flock (the people around us we are seeking to reach). Who are they? What are their needs? Where are they hurting that could be a point of contact with them for the sake of the gospel? How can we access their world in a relevant, yet uncompromising way? How can we mobilize our people to build relationships with them and share the gospel?

In this light, there can be no substitute for a practical, prayerful process of annual strategic planning. Every pastor ought to become a student of how to think through the big picture of the church—where the church is, where it needs to go, and a clear strategy to get there. He needs to understand how to involve people in that process. And then he must be good at casting God's discovered vision to the church.

If godly leaders realize that a pastor is just creating direction or programming "on a whim" without God's initiation, he's in real trouble. Also, if they see that he is not thinking clearly about the overall picture, he will lose credibility. If he sees something that's wrong, but doesn't explain the need for change in light of God's vision for the church, he will find himself losing ground. It won't make sense to people.

Why is this so important? Many conflicts could have been avoided if the lead pastor and elders had learned how to find God's vision through careful, strategic thinking and then addressed issues in light of that vision.

I can say to my son, "Son, get up and move this furniture." Now, he should do it because I'm his dad, but it might make no sense to him. If I said, "Son, we've been thinking about it and have bought a pool table so you and your friends can hang out here. We need to get this furniture moved so we can get that pool table in here." With that vision, he'll leap off the floor!

People are not idiots. They need to understand the rationale behind why we are asking for change. Without this knowledge, navigating change becomes far more difficult.

There are some good tools available regarding the art of strategic planning. One of the best is the book, *Masterplanning,* by Bobb Biehl (a must read). As Biehl illustrates, any process you employ should start from the end result and work backward and should include the components listed below. (The following incorporates a little variation of Biehl's Masterplanning Arrow technique.)

NEEDS: What needs do we see around us that we are passionate about or uniquely called to accomplish?

MISSION: In light of those needs, what is our mission? What is it we are called to do?

MINISTRY AREAS: What are the specific ministries we must employ to accomplish this mission? Most churches need ministries in the areas of worship, equipping, missions, age-appropriate ministries, etc.

OBJECTIVES: What are the broad areas we must give attention to in each ministry? These may be things such as training leaders, communication to the team, events, small group work, etc.

STRATEGIES: What are the specific strategies/programs we will use this year or on an ongoing basis?

GOALS: What are the measurable, reachable goals we will use for emphasis and evaluation this year?

CALENDAR AND BUDGET: When will we do this and how much will it cost? These are the final components of a good masterplan. Your church budget and calendar should always rise as a reflection of your mission and the process you have developed before God to reach that mission.

(In appendix B you will find a sample tool for this master-plannng process.)

Regardless of what model or process you employ, as a good leader you must learn how to lead your people to see the mission, develop strategies before God that will accomplish that mission, and then cast vision to that end.

As that process begins to unfold you may find opposition to those plans. If you have done your work well and brought along a majority of leaders with you who have helped develop the vision, you will find that they are supportive. Those who do not will find themselves opposing what has logically and prayerfully been developed.

The bottom line is this: You can avoid many battles and preclude a lot of problems by moving by God's initiation (with the aid of God's Word, Spirit, and godly counselors). You can also avoid a lot of battles by careful, prayerful strategic planning that begins with the mission and vision that God has given you.

But notice that I said you can avoid "many" battles this way. Not all. You will discover that finding God's initiatives often *creates* conflict with some. When you feel you have found God's clear path for your church and people still will not follow, and are even belligerent in their opposition, what do you do?

Navigating Opposition

There once was a man in a church I pastored who had come out of a quasi-Christian cult on a college campus. He said to me, "Bill, I love this church because I think it is so New Testament in its makeup." I thanked him for the compliment but asked him what he thought was so biblical about it. To my amazement he replied, "Because there are so many carnal people in it!"

I was shocked…and then really wanted to know what he meant. He said, "In a cult, everyone is either 100% committed or they are out. That's not the model I see in the scripture of the church. The Bible indicates there is usually a committed core, but there are also concentric circles of commitment. Some are growing, but not there. Some are just beginning their walk with Christ and very immature. Some are just on the fringes looking in. The New Testament church is not a club of perfect Christians, but a growing family of people at all stages of development." Great insight.

I have eight children. Eight. It makes me tired just writing that number! Four strong boys and four beautiful girls. We've had kids in every age group in the church for years. My wife is incredible and has done a great job with our kids. Together we've had the privilege and awesome responsibility of raising these crumb-grabbers for Christ and by God's grace they are already making great impact for His kingdom.

If I am going to shepherd them well through their lives I must understand the stages of their development and accept them there. I don't want my 13-year-old trying to act like my 32-year-old or vice versa. There are certain things my younger kids do that are explainable in terms of their youth and immaturity. I don't need to discipline them for acts of childishness. I may need to speak to them about it, but not discipline. However, as they grow and there are clear acts of disobedience or rebellion in areas where they know better and are able to handle, I must address it.

Every church is like a family. We have people at all stages of growth. As good fathers in the faith we should expect more mature thinking and behavior from the older believers. Those who are younger or weaker in the faith should be dealt with accordingly. This is why Paul addresses multiple issues when he says, "admonish the unruly, encourage the fainthearted, help the weak, be patient with everyone" (1 Thessalonians 5:14).

But there are times we have people in our church who are obstinate and willful in their sin or opposition. There are clear processes we are to employ to deal with sinning believers in a way that treats them with dignity and love, but firm truth. Almost every book of the New Testament has something to say about this. The following is not a full discussion of spiritual restoration—or the process we often call "church discipline"—but rather a few thoughts on how this process applies to moments of church conflict.

Perhaps the most comprehensive passage about how to deal with a sinning brother or sister is found in Matthew, Chapter 18. There we are given a process that begins with a private conversation. This may be the most frequently violated command in Scripture! One of the most grievous errors a pastor can make is to see one member responding in a sinful way and then choose to "shotgun" the whole church with a scathing sermon the next week, or go and talk to others, rather than dealing with them directly. That's a cowardly approach. If you see a believer who is overtaken in a sin, then you should go to them and appeal to them in private. Very often issues are resolved when this approach is taken.

If the individual is a true believer they will generally respond positively to loving, prayerful, gentle conversation. If they fail to respond to this and their sin becomes more deliberate—even public—and is creating conflict, then the Word gives further instruction about how to work through the process. Always the goal is to preserve the reputation of God, the health of the church body, and hopefully, the restoration of the individual.

The pastor and church leaders must always take several things into consideration:

1. Is this issue so significant that it should be confronted or is it something that will work itself out in time? Is it a symptom of immaturity or belligerent rebellion?

2. Is what they are doing hindering the health and progress of the church? Are they influencing others? Is gossip involved (which is one of the main cancers of the church)? Is this so significant that, unless addressed, it will abort the church fulfilling its God-initiated mission?

3. Is this an issue of preference or principle? Some people may be doing some things I don't like or agree with, but I have no biblical grounds for my disagreement. It's just a matter of personal preference. But if they are doing something that is violating a biblical principle, and it is affecting the life of the church, it may need to be addressed. Or if they are holding the church hostage to their preferences, confusing them with biblical principles, this too must be confronted.

4. Am I anxious to confront this because it is bothering me personally? Perhaps people are not accepting my leadership or they simply don't like me (it happens)! I must make sure that any confrontation that I initiate must be because God is leading there, and not because I'm hurt personally and want a little revenge.

5. Is it the right time to address this? There are a myriad of considerations here.

- Do I have enough leadership capital to pull this off without simply being alone? (Although there are times when I must confront issues even if I am the only one who sees it.)
- Have we done a proper job of bringing people along with the vision to the extent that there is really no legitimate reason for their concerns? In other words, are their concerns a matter of willful, sinful disobedience against God or simply because we have not done a good job of communication?
- Is there a major initiative on the agenda that needs our focus? Should this be addressed later after we move the church

forward in the next step of the vision? Or, is what's happening with this individual or group something that is directly impending the vision and must be dealt with now?

This is tough. No question about it. The timing of confronting opposition must be determined through the leadership of the Spirit, the counsel of godly leaders, and a huge dose of sanctified common sense.

But sometimes conflict comes right at you and you must deal with it—and it cannot be avoided. At these moments you have no choice but to take the necessary time and energy to address the issue.

I was one year into a new pastorate and discovered that a very prominent leader was having an affair with a young lady in our church. We began the process of sifting through the problem and trying to help. God's process is very clear, but sin always makes things messy. The individuals involved would not admit their sin and covered it in a very confusing way. It was a rough moment.

I called my middle brother, Jim, who has always been a great counselor to me, and began to do a little spiritualized whining.

"Things were going so great," I moaned. "Why did this have to happen now?"

I'll never forget what Jim said. "Bill, this isn't an intrusion to pastoring; this IS pastoring."

If you aren't willing to deal with opposition you better find another job. We're all sinful. Sin causes conflicts. Pastoring people through that process is an essential part of their development and yours.

And there's that thing called "love"...

This is really hard for us to swallow, but sometimes as leaders one of the main problems in the midst of opposition is our simple lack of love for our people. In the excellent book, *Leadership and*

Self-Deception by the Arbinger Institute, the authors point out that conflict often occurs because we treat people like objects and not people. We have a goal and vision of where we're headed. People become merely a means to that goal. This lack of biblical love can always be felt, whether someone can verbalize what's happening or not. When people feel this manipulation they will react. The issue itself becomes immaterial.

As you face the conflict in your congregation, you must first make sure that you are allowing the God of love within you to fill and flood your heart with His love—that you are allowing the love of God to be "shed abroad in your heart by the Holy Spirit" (Romans 5:5). Such love is not natural but is a fruit made available to us by the Holy Spirit who resides within (Galatians 5:22; 1 John 4:7-8). This may take a process of resolving some past hurts to open up room for His love to flow, which we will take about later, but it must be done.

Paul says that without the love of God ruling and reigning in our hearts all we are is nothing, all we do amounts to nothing, and all we receive from what we do is nothing (1 Corinthians 13:1-3). Pretty important. If you face conflict and opposition with no love, you will always fail. You may be dead right in your conclusions, but lethally wrong in your application. And if you find yourself in a position where someone must be biblically confronted, you cannot do that properly without the love of God really flowing fully through your life.

But when my heart is filled with God's love (and your people know it), your mind is filled with His vision (and you've discovered and communicated it faithfully and well) and there is still conflict, then you know it's time to courageously address the issue head-on.

Navigation Gate #5:

- Take your list developed in Navigation Gate #1. With trusted leaders, come up with a biblical game plan for dealing with each issue. What are the next biblical steps to take?
- If you have not done a good job of strategic planning, begin to study and implement this process. Don't hesitate to enlist another pastor's help or an outside consultant. Too much is at stake to do this poorly.

From: Matt Johnson
To: Jim Bradford
CC:
Subject: confidential

Dear Jim,

O.K., I hate to even bring this up and I trust that you'll keep this between me and you. But I am finding myself battling a lot of fear. It looks like we're facing an unavoidable battle. I've done everything I know to bring this along properly and handle it gracefully, but I have some folks that will not give it a rest. It's very apparent to our key leaders that if this is not confronted and resolved we'll never fulfill our destiny as a church. I feel like the soul of the church is at stake.

I also know that if I weigh in it's going to cost me. Not only with my members, but I'm wondering what my friends and colleagues are going to say about me. Things were going pretty well and I was getting some nice commendation for my work and that could all come to a screeching halt.

As I write these words I want to take them back because they sound so stinkin' petty and self-serving. But I can't. It's real. It's in me. And I don't know what to do about it.

Matt

- -

From: Jim Bradford
To: Matt Johnson
CC:
Subject: RE: confidential

Dear Matt,

I can't tell you how encouraged I am by your honesty. Every leader has had to face this issue. In fact, for most of us, it is one of the defining moments of our lives.

In the midst of my first leadership challenge, God rolled back the curtain and showed me how much I lived for man's approval. I was gripped with a major man-fearing spirit and didn't even know it. Really painful and humiliating.

Seeing that and letting God deal with it, though, brought liberation to my life in ways I can hardly describe. I've often wondered if the whole purpose of the exercise in that first conflict was more for me than the church.

I'm enclosing some further thoughts about this. Get a cup of coffee—maybe a whole pot—and sit down to think deeply. This is a lifelong issue, but right now it sounds like it's time for the initial surgery!

The patient in the bed beside you!

Jim

CHAPTER SIX

OVERCOMING FEAR

"What if they reject me?"

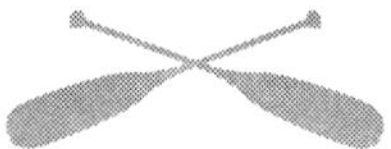

He was a strong man and had been the chairman of everything before I came. Most people in the church equated his high involvement with deep spirituality. But underneath this thin veneer was a bitter man who loved to be in charge. His involvement was simply a means of control. There were no decisions made in the church that this man did not feel he was entitled to direct. He spoke up in every business meeting and leadership council and always had an agenda.

When I came to the church I naively believed that he was just a very involved layman. Pastors love men who engage and this man was everywhere. Very soon I came to see the motivations behind his activity and the depth of his controlling, demanding spirit. He could smile at you, mow you down with his eyes, and level you with a laser remark that made you know that if he was crossed there would consequences—all at the same time! And it was always couched in spiritual words, sort of like some Pharisees I'd read about.

As a young pastor full of ideas and passion, I saw all of the changes that needed to occur and set out in those directions. Like-minded believers were behind me and we began to make progress. But our controlling friend would always voice his concerns. I found myself, in the name of unity and peace, deferring to him more than once in areas that I really didn't agree with. Often a well-intentioned leader would say, "Well, we could do that, but you know what Fred* will say" (*not his real name).

His control grew stronger, influencing us all. I knew that to stand against him in any arena would cost me relationally with him and a host of his followers. Without even realizing it, I became tentative in my leadership and missed some key opportunities. It got worse and worse. He constantly questioned my motives and authority and quietly spread discord among others.

One day, as I was complaining to the Lord about this man, I sensed He was showing me I was literally letting this man lead the church! I was allowing his controlling bitterness to direct the entire body of believers. This was not his fault, it was mine. I was abdicating my God-given responsibility to lead and there was one reason which I was about to discover.

In an intense season of prayer for the church we scheduled a two-week meeting with Life Action Ministries to seek God for revival. I fasted and prayed. God came and that two-week meeting extended every night for four weeks! People were saved and lives were forever changed in what was one of the greatest spiritual movements in a church that I've witnessed in my lifetime. Pride and all its manifestations was gracefully exposed by the Lord. Unforgiveness and bitterness came to the surface and was released. Fifty people were saved and there was never an evangelistic message preached. More than 250 people headed to the prayer room enmasse one night as God exposed and purged sins of immorality and impurity. God brought fresh brokenness and surrender to our church. Our friend and his followers, though, were conspicuously absent.

But the greatest change was to come to me. I sat on the front row every night and said, "Lord, before revival comes to this church, I need it to come in my heart." One night, the Lord decided it was time to uncover the groundwork of my soul. The preacher was speaking on pride—the mother of all sins. Slowly the precious Physician lifted his scalpel and began his life-saving surgery.

"Why is it that you have such a desire to be liked?"

"Why is it you seek everyone's approval on everything?"

"Why do you refuse to make the tough decisions at times?"

"Why are you upset when your wife doesn't tell you what a great job you did preaching as you travel home on Sunday morning?"

"Why will you not confront "Fred?" (the bitter, controlling man)

"Why have you lived your life longing to be the center of attention?"

"Why, when other pastors are talking about their church or sermons, do you subtly steer the conversation to your church and what you have accomplished?"

"Why do you want people to notice your success?"

"Why are you so afraid of failure?"

"Why do you always have an excuse for your failures?"

"Why are you so quick to defend yourself and so slow to applaud others?"

"Why do you blame others so often?"

...and on and on it went. It was strong, but sweet. Deep, but so gracious that I was willing to hear it all. Del Fehsenfeld of Life Action was preaching. While he was still speaking, I moved to my knees and soon found myself face down on the carpet weeping and realizing there was one answer to all of those questions: PRIDE.

I hope I never get over that moment. That realization was a watershed for my spiritual growth. One of the greatest manifestations of pride in my life was a man-fearing, man-pleasing spirit. We all long to be approved of, liked, loved, admired, honored. There is actually nothing wrong with a passion to be loved. In fact, I believe it was placed in us by God to drive us to Him. But when we look to men to fulfill that need—instead of God alone—we become enslaved to the fear of man, which emasculates leadership.

"Wishing to satisfy the crowd, Pilate...handed Jesus over to be crucified" (Mark 15:15).

Whoever you fear you will serve. If you fear nothing but God alone, you will do whatever He says without hesitation. If you fear man, you may end up crucifying Christ.

Overcoming the real source of fear

Courage is the non-negotiable of leadership. Those who lead don't point in the right direction—they go ahead of others leading them there. The potential for fear is constant when you have to go first, are responsible for those who follow, and carry the weight for wrong decisions. You also realize that even if you take the right steps many may disagree and think less of you. If you are unwilling to face and deal with these fears you are not a candidate for leadership.

To become "dis-couraged" is to lose your courage. In ministry, discouragement is a constant demon lurking behind every decision, every conversation, every step. You don't even have to do anything to be overwhelmed with this monster. The demons of discouragement can mount your back on Monday morning before you get out of bed.

If you allow the fear of man to dominate your heart it will become your master. It will make decisions for you, taking you places you never intended to go. This silent enemy can stop a well-meaning leader dead in his tracks. *"I wanted to suggest that move, take that step, but...."*

The greatest fear for most leaders is not a concern about taking people to the wrong places. It is a fear of *what people will think* if he takes them in the wrong directions or even the right directions. So we stall in leadership. We can make this sound righteous and holy, a desire for "peace" in the body, etc. In reality, it is often merely our pride that makes us unwilling to make a hard choice, oppose ungodliness, and lead courageously because we know we may lose approval. And we *love* approval.

Like any other sin, when we seek to fulfill a legitimate desire (to be loved) in an illegitimate way (by men instead of God alone) we always fail. When we look to man for recognition instead of God, we are in trouble. Not only does it abort our spiritual leadership, it never satisfies…and we keep running down a path that has no finish line. I know men who have used up their lives and shipwrecked churches simply by "looking for love in all the wrong places." In reality, the fear of man is nothing more than the love of self.

When our primary goal is to have everyone like us, it seriously alters our decision-making. No longer is our goal the glory of God... it is the honor and acceptance of ME. This can be amazingly subtle for spiritual leaders because we can couch all of our directives in spiritual-sounding terms when our motivation is anything but biblical.

How do we slay this leadership killer? How do we overcome a man-fearing spirit? How do we rise above dis-couragement?

First, we must become secure in God's ever-lasting love. "Perfect love casts out fear" (1 John 4:18b), is not a statement about our relationships with others. The Apostle John is relaying to us the security that comes when we finally understand God loves us unconditionally. We don't have to prove anything to Him to be loved by Him. Even His discipline (training) of us is an act of love. It is hard for us to grasp the comprehensiveness of this love because our human experience is so tainted with partiality. But God is perfect. His love is the same both in quality and quantity. When we become secure in the position we have before God we no longer have to prove anything to anyone.

Michael Jordan was the greatest basketball player of the 20th century: hands down. If we were on a backyard court and he walked up to play with us, we would make him one of the captains. If he picked you, you wouldn't care what anyone else thought. "He picked ME," you would shout. "Can you believe it? He must see something in me that he values." You wouldn't be concerned about what anyone else thought about your athletic abilities because you had been chosen by the best. His opinion slam-dunks everyone else's.

Don't look for Michael Jordan in your neighborhood anytime soon, but understand something far greater has already transpired.

> *"...He chose us in Him before the foundation of the world... He predestined us to adoption as sons through Jesus Christ to Himself" (Ephesians 1:4-5).*

You were picked by God. He loves you with an "ever" lasting love and is eternally committed to "conform you to the image of His Son" (Romans 8:29). If you had an earthly father or mother with any semblance of this kind of unconditional love, you know what it means to rest in that approval. John, the beloved apostle, said we "...have come to know and have believed the love God has for us" (1 John 4:16). Those who know and really believe this are so secure that they don't have to seek approval anywhere else. "The Lord is for me, what can man do to me?" (Psalm 118:6).

Secure in this love, we must die to what others think. When Jesus was giving the simple requirements for discipleship, he made a comparative statement that is startling at first glance.

> *"If anyone comes to Me and does not hate his own father and mother and wife and children and brothers and sisters, yes, and even his own life, he cannot be My disciple" (Luke 14:26).*

Obviously Christ was not calling for family hatred. But what he was calling for was a willingness to die to what others thought. A death to your reputation. If you study this passage in Luke 14:25-33, you will discover three areas where we must come to total surrender: our relationships, our possessions, and our physical bodies. If you have not died there, you will be open to continual temptation. When you die to what others think of you, you can lead. If others follow, that's wonderful. If you have gone where God asks and others do not follow, you still see His smile.

I often have to remind myself that I have an audience of One. My goal is to please and honor Him. If I do that, any accolades that He thinks I need from men will come my way. If I have not died to my reputation I will find myself constantly adjusting my decisions to gain man's applause. A great leader lives for the applause of heaven.

I must choose to live for a higher reward. Eternity is a long time and heaven is a real place. When I live with a strong eternal perspective, I am willing to lose a few temporary cheers from men and wait for what's soon to come.

The Great Reward

Paul was loved by the people who mattered most but hated by a lot of his contemporaries. He was beaten three times, stoned and left for dead once, and run out of almost every town in which he ministered. It's safe to assume that very little would have been accomplished if Paul had been stopped by the fear of man. We might not even know his name. But 2,000 years later he is loved and appreciated by everyone who names Christ's name. And most importantly, he is standing right now before the One whose opinion makes all the difference. "In the future," Paul mused, "there is laid up for me a crown of righteousness which the LORD, the righteous judge, will award to me on that day; and not only to me, but also to all who have loved His appearing" (1 Timothy 4:8).

Imagine the scene. The great expanse of heaven is filled with all the believers from all of time. Surrounding us are the billions of angels and created beings in their perfection. Before us there is a throne and One seated on it with His glorious Son at His right hand. It is time for rewards. We're not in a hurry. We've waited all our lives for this and we have all of eternity to enjoy it.

Paul is called up for his reward. A murmur begins and grows to a roar as everyone speculates on what the great Apostle will receive. Paul humbly comes to stand before the King and God motions for him to turn and face the crowd.

"Paul, do you remember me?" a young man cries out. "I'm Timothy. You led me to Christ and invested in me. I'm here, Paul, by the grace of God as it came through you."

Suddenly the crowd erupts in applause. The angels start singing with the most glorious symphony ever heard, far greater than any earthly music. It goes on and on.

After awhile, another lady stands.

"Paul, I know you may not remember, but I'm Lydia. While others passed by, you stopped at the lake and explained the way of God to my friends and me. We're all here today because of God and His work through you." (A whole group of ladies stand with her.)

"And by the way, Paul, here are my children," (they stand) "and their children," (they stand) "and their children's children who have come to Christ because of your influence."

Suddenly a ripple of people begins to rise—all of Lydia and Paul's spiritual descendants—hundreds and then thousands and then millions as the crowd explodes in a deafening roar of affirmation and wonder.

This goes on for hours, days, as one after another voices their gratitude. Those who came to Christ through Paul's fearless preaching and those who repented because of his rebuke and confrontation, all join the chorus. Paul is reminded of the very words he wrote under the inspiration of the Holy Spirit years before. They now explode with full understanding in his mind. "For who is our hope or joy or crown of exultation? Is it not even you in the presence of our Lord Jesus at His coming? For you are our glory and joy" (1 Thessalonians 2:19-20).

Finally, the crowd grows quiet and every eye is on the Father. He lays his hand on Paul's shoulder and turns him around. The mere touch sends a wave of unexplainable joy coursing through Paul's entire glorified body. And then the words come as God's eyes penetrate Paul's soul.

"Well done, my son. You are a good and faithful servant. Enter into the joy I have prepared for you before the foundation of the world!"

Enough. It is enough. What men have said or not said—their opinions and their human evaluations. The criticism, gossip, beatings, stoning, and the abuse from others is forever washed away in the fullness of the Father's love.

Don't worry what people think. The most important applause will soon begin.

NAVIGATION GATE #6:

- Spend an extended time in prayerful evaluation and record any areas of pride or man-fearing that God reveals to you. Invite a trusted friend or counselor to help in this evaluation and confess any revealed failure to God.

From: Matt Johnson
To: Jim Bradford
CC:
Subject: Whole lot of confusion

Dear Jim,

I'm sorry for pestering you so much, but I guess I am feeling pretty lonely. I want to cry with Elijah, "I alone am left a prophet in Israel," and crawl up under a tree. Maybe I'm just wallowing in a little self-pity.

What's most troubling to me though is that I have a lot of good men around me who are confused. They are being pulled by the questions of long-time friends. I feel I may be losing some of them. If anything is going to be built here, I have to have the guys all headed in the right direction. I even have good men wondering about my leadership, I think. Without them, it's going to be pretty hopeless. Is there any way to gather the troops together?

Confused myself,

Matt

- -

From: Jim Bradford
To: Matt Johnson
CC:
Subject: RE: Whole lot of confusion

Dear Matt,

You have now joined the ranks of Elijah, David, Peter and a few other heroes who had moments of great loneliness in leadership. It's not easy. Take a look at Jesus in Gethsemane. What you do with this is critical. If you don't seize this moment and handle it properly it could be very detrimental, not only to you, but the direction you desire to head.

You've got to build a core of men who will stand for what's right. Without that, not only will you be alone, but your church will never make the turn to positive, God-led change for His glory. I've always found this begins with the men... and you.

On your team,

Jim

CHAPTER SEVEN

BUILDING THE CORE

"Who will stand with me?"

It was a massacre that could have been avoided. The infamous Battle of the Little Bighorn, led by General George Armstrong Custer, occurred in Montana territory on June 25 and 26, 1876. Custer's battalion of 700 troops was unaware that a coalition of more than 2,000 Lakota and Cheyenne Indians had been formed under the visionary leadership of Chief Sitting Bull.

Custer was an aggressive cavalry officer and felt that the greatest plan of battle was to attack the Indians before they scattered. He felt this even against repeated warnings by his Indian scouts that the Indian camp was the largest they had ever seen in 30 years. Officers tried to persuade him to take the Gatlin guns, but Custer was afraid they would slow him down. He also refused offers of additional troops, assuring other officers that his troops could "handle anything." What would occur next was the second greatest loss of military soldiers in any engagement of the expansion into the West (more than 250 men).

All of this could have been avoided if Custer had not underestimated his enemy's strength and waited on necessary reinforcements.

It is a noble step to attempt to redeem a church. When a pastor is called to the task it is a high honor…a great privilege. But it can be a battle. As in any engagement, a good leader must think strategically and never underestimate the forces that stand against kingdom advancement.

If you are to see significant change come in the life of a church you must have the cavalry riding over the hill at just the right moments. Any pastor who tries to be a lone ranger may lie on the battlefield like Custer, with mortal wounds and very little progress.

This is why it is essential to capture the hearts of the male leadership in the church. Obviously, you must seek to lead everyone in the church in the direction God is indicating. But of particular importance is the engagement of the men. If the men see the value of change and embrace it, most of their wives will follow. If they do not, you have no help. Also, if a pastor concentrates on convincing only the women of the plans he is seeking, without involving the men, he is headed for deep trouble.

Creating Clarity

How do you give men a great vision for the expansion of God's kingdom and prepare them for the necessary battles along the way? I would suggest three primary approaches. You can do this in many different ways, but it's all about discipling men—personally, in small groups, and in larger gatherings.

In my second full-time church after seminary the Lord blessed us with tremendous growth very quickly. We realized that if we didn't develop leaders we were going to have an inverted and very unstable leadership pyramid. We needed to train men and train them fast.

I had already been seeking to disciple men one at a time. Having been greatly influenced by others in this biblical approach it was natural to me. Over coffee or lunch or at random times, the Lord had given me the privilege of investing in men individually. We memorized scripture, talked about our problems, and looked at the future and where we felt God wanted to take us. We just lived life together.

One of the greatest verses on discipleship to me is recorded the day Jesus appointed his first apostles. After a night of prayer He "appointed twelve that they would *be with Him* and he would send them out to preach" (Mark 3:14). Christ's method of training men was simple, but strategic. He was with them. When they wondered about their finances He talked to them about the lilies of the field and they watched how He trusted His Father. They observed how He paid His taxes. They learned how to relate to people by watching him engage a small tax gatherer up in a tree. They grew in their love by seeing Him stoop down to talk to a woman caught in adultery and converse with a Samaritan woman by a well. They became like Him as they walked with Him.

Any leader who desires change must disciple men. It must not be a duty, but something at the core of his DNA—as natural as breathing and as constant. Men will not live and die for a leader they don't know. And you cannot build a church without building men.

Also, you must train men in small groups. I had already begun a small, early morning bible study / prayer / accountability group. In retrospect, I don't know how this happened other than the leadership of the Lord, but that group continued for ten years. It was open to anyone, but consisted of about 25 men who would come at various times and ten men who were there without fail. I don't know if it was the camaraderie or the coffee and donuts, but something amazing happened in that group over time. I would begin with a question that helped us get to know each other followed by a short time of teaching (often out of my devotional time). Then I would lead them into discussion and group prayer and we would be promptly finished in an hour. Often, we never got past the opening question as God began to do His work.

A lot of life change happened in that group. Very soon our hearts began to be knit together in love. Like David's mighty men, we came to a point where we would live and die for each other.

Out of that group we began to sense a need for a larger concentration of men to be developed. I appealed to the elected leaders in that congregationally led church and about half of them decided to join us. This appeal was necessary, but I was not surprised by the response of those who didn't join. I wanted them to join us, but I knew some wouldn't. But I wanted all the current leaders to realize they were given the chance to become a greater leader. After that I opened the monthly training time up for all the men of the church and challenged them with a big vision. I was hoping to have 25 men to train.

When the Wednesday night meeting came, I was shocked to walk into a room of 95 hungry men! I had to change my approach quickly, but over the next three years we met monthly, then weekly and built an incredible core of godly men, by the grace of God.

In subsequent churches I have always felt that real strength in a church comes by building this core. This must not be a passive engagement with men, but an aggressive, strategic plan to raise up men who know God, understand His Word, and know how to lead courageously. It must not be a duty, a chore, or simply something the pastor feels he has to do to accomplish an agenda. It should be at the root of his life to help his men grow and become mighty men for God's glory.

Today there are a number of good materials available. *Men's Fraternity*, Robert Lewis' three-year training program for men, is one of the best. It appeals to men through the portal of their manhood which is a great draw. Every man wants to understand what a real man is, which is covered in the first year. They are led through the scripture to adopt a definition of manhood as one who does the following: "Resists passivity, accepts responsibility, leads courageously, and lives for a greater reward."

The remaining two years teach a man how to be a leader in his family, his work, and then in the particular areas of ministry—the Great Adventure—God has called him to. Great stuff. Regardless of what material or approach you use, you must train men and the pastor should be leading the charge.

Why is training of men so essential? You need the cavalry. Every church must realize they are in an all-out battle against " rulers, against the power, against the world forces of this darkness, against the spiritual forces of wickedness in the heavenly places" (Ephesians 6:12).

Along with that, there are often "tares sown among the wheat" in the church. These are lost church members who will often give great opposition as was mentioned earlier. And there lies within every person, even believers, the potential for selfishness and sinful responses. Leading any church involves a proper assessment of the forces that might oppose God's direction and the proper troops to achieve God's kind of success.

The Residual of Discipleship

After three years of training the men in the church I mentioned, we encountered some serious opposition to change. The church was growing and some men were losing their positions of influence because the bar had been raised on the standards for authentic leadership. New, godly leaders had joined the church. Aspiring leaders, both young and old, were rising up. Some of the "old guard" leaders had held their position simply by the past vacuum of leadership. When they realized they were losing their power and authority the battle was on.

As a young, naive pastor filled with vision I assumed they would eventually come around if given time. Months and months of opposition gradually dispelled that assumption. The battle got intense. The stakes were high. I was trying to lead the best I knew, but I felt very alone in my job.

I remember one night telling my wife that if the cavalry didn't come over the hill we were sunk. I was willing to die on that hill because it was one that was of value. God's word and reputation were at stake. He had called me there and I must lead. But it would be nice if there were some reinforcements.

God waited until the midnight hour (perhaps testing and training me) but at precisely the right moment our men stood up. These were the men of my early morning men's group, our large group training times, and the men I had eaten with, wept with, envisioned ministry with, grown with. They stood together and in a beautiful display of grace and truth, protected the church and led us through one of the most critical battles of her history. It was a hard but beautiful thing to watch.

I never feel quite so alive as a man or a leader as when I am engaged in a battle for a great, essential cause. It's never easy and I cry for escape at times, but there is a sense of nobility about such seasons. And when a band of brothers surrounds you, it is one of the highest moments of your existence on this earth.

&

The hour was bleak. It was the most intense battle in human history. So great was the struggle that even the best men ran to the hills in humiliation and retreat. When the great Leader looked down almost everyone was gone. He alone stood impaled upon a Roman cross, waging the war for the souls of all those who would be redeemed for all the ages.

But a few days later, at just the right moment, reinforcements came. His Father lifted Him from the grave with resurrection power. His disciples were still around—scared, confused, but there nonetheless—and with a little more discipling and the same dose of resurrection power, they were ready to lead the assault against the forces of hell. Two thousand years later, millions of lives have been saved, rescued by this valiant Leader and his Kingdom troops called the church.

You are a part of this band of brothers…this noble cause…this great adventure. And you are not alone.

Navigation Gate #7:

- Make a list of the men you know are standing with you. Get them together for coffee and read through this chapter aloud. Let them help you develop further plans for developing men in your church and thank them for their invaluable role. Help them to see their vital importance in the church's future.

From: Matt Johnson
To: Jim Bradford
CC:
Subject: The gossip train has left the station

Dear Jim,

It's getting pretty crazy here. Rumors are flying around. Gossip is everywhere. I'm hearing stuff coming back to me about what I said and did that is amazing and totally false.

What's incredible is that, if they wanted to, there's a lot of stuff they could accuse me of that would be accurate! But it seems that their charges are leveled at things that are not based in fact at all.

It's tearing up the church. It's like watching a tornado storm through a town and sucking more and more people into its vortex. What I'd like to do is haul out a sermonic shotgun this Sunday and give 'em both barrels. But that wouldn't be good... right???

How do I stop the talk?

Matt

- -

From: Jim Bradford
To: Matt Johnson
CC:
Subject: RE: The gossip train has left the station

Dear Matt,

Sadly, what you're experiencing is fairly normal for this kind of experience. Gossip is Satan's sucker punch to the church. I've seen more churches worn down and knocked out by these continual jabs than any other device. I know you are realizing this, but this can get really nasty...and painful.

There are both reactive and proactive steps for you to take in this moment and the enclosed document will cover both. I believe they will help you navigate the whitewater.

And remember...regardless of what people say, what God says is what matters. Follow Him explicitly and you'll come out on top.

Praying,

Jim

CHAPTER EIGHT

HANDLING GOSSIP

"Can I stop the talk?"

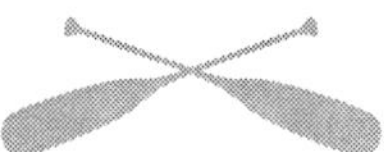

They called it Black Friday. The worst fire in the recorded history of Yellowstone National Park began in the summer of 1988 with record drought conditions. A total of 248 separate fires blazed which 25,000 firefighters attacked, at a total cost of more than $120 million.

Black Friday, August 20, 1988 was the worst day as high winds pushed the fire over 150,000 acres and shot flames 20 stories (200 feet) into the air. The day turned as black as night as the smoke billowed and ash drifted as far as Billings, Montana over 60 miles away. On that single day more land was consumed than by all other fires combined since the establishment of the park.

"Wildfire" is a term used to describe an uncontrolled combustion that occurs in wilderness areas. It can travel at speeds up to fifteen miles per hour and, if left unchecked, can continue for months. The great fire in Yellowstone began in June and continued until snows slowed—and finally stopped—its spread in November.

What's so destructive about wildfire is its ability to jump gaps, change directions, and move at incredible speeds too fast for humans to control. And it doesn't take much to start. A cigarette, a lightning strike, an arcing power line. It just takes a small ignition to a combustible source to create massive damage.

Gossip is the wildfire of church conflict and there's nothing so destructive.

"See how great a forest is set aflame by such a small fire! And the tongue is a fire, the very world of iniquity; the tongue is set among our members that which defiles the entire body and is set on fire by hell" (James 3:5-6)

It can spread at record speeds, jump gaps of truth, and decimate both individual lives and the witness of an entire church in the community for years. It is one of Satan's greatest tools in his attack against God's church.

The church is the representation of God in a community. Christ is the head and we are the body. Just as He carried out His work in the flesh through the instrument of His human body, so are we now that expression to the world. Jesus said about His human existence, "If you've seen me, you've seen the Father" (Johh 14:9). This is exactly what is to happen through every local church. Jonathan Edwards said our goal as believers and as a church is to "give the world a right opinion of God."

The church is to be a walking, living, breathing, loving expression of the life of God. It is the precursor to heaven and the picture of that perfect community. "I've never seen people who love each other so greatly, who care for each other's needs, who respect one another, who treat each other with such compassion and dignity. I wish I could be a part of a community like that," should be the comments we hear. The church should make unbelievers thirsty for God and for the possibility of living eternally in a place of perfect love.

That's why gossip is so deadly. It destroys that picture and gives the world a grotesque caricature of God. When we slander and gossip we are destroying the unity, not of an organization, but of the living, breathing body of Christ. This is why Paul is so adamant that we should "work diligently to preserve the unity of the Spirit in the bond of peace" (Ephesians 4:3).

Gossip "separates intimate friends" by forever changing our opinion of their character (Proverbs 20:19). It destroys the interrelationships of the cells in the Body, making the church susceptible to every passing disease.

And it comes from one source: pride. Josiah Holland said, "One of the most amazing things is what gossip reveals about a person. Gossip is always a personal confession either of malice or imbecility."

Those who gossip are airing their dirty laundry for the "mouth speaks out of that which fills the heart" (Matthew 12:34). When we slander others it manifests a heart so arrogant it must let people know our supposed superiority. "Did you see what she did?" is another way of saying "I would never do that. I'm better than her." "I'm glad I'm not like other men," said the Pharisee.

It's also amazingly hypocritical. We point out a supposed sin in others as we commit a sin ourselves! At church it can be spread in terms that make it even sound spiritual. "I'm not trying to gossip, but we really need to be praying for ________. Why, I heard that he…"

God has a low opinion about those who engage in this assault against His children and His body.

> *"He who spreads slander is a fool" (Proverbs 11:18b).*

> *"There are six things which the Lord hates, yes, seven which are an abomination to Him: haughty eyes, a lying tongue, and hands that shed innocent blood; a heart that devises wicked plans, feet that run rapidly to evil, a false witness who utters lies and one who spreads strife among others" (Proverbs 6:16-19).*

Notice that every single statement in the Proverbs passage above is present in those who gossip! When you talk about my children it affects me deeply. God is no different and He is absolutely righteous in His opinion. God hates gossip and what it does to His family.

Controlling Wildfire

Every good firefighter knows there are both proactive and reactive approaches dealing with wildfire. A good leader in God's kingdom must understand the same.

Proactively we must seek to stop the fires of gossip before they begin. This can be done in several ways.

Compelling Communication: People want and need to know what's going on. When church leaders fail to communicate properly it opens the door for speculation and concern. Sometimes these concerns are legitimate and often they are not, but you can't fault people for wanting to know about the direction of the church.

Consistent Vision: Good leaders cast vision. They do it clearly and often. Andy Stanley has pointed out that vision leaks and it must be repeated over and over again for the majority of a church community to grasp.

Of course, there must BE vision. If the leaders, and subsequently the church, lose a compelling cause to live and die for they will revert to selfishness. The natural flow of a visionless church is inward. Good leaders head this off at the pass by finding God-initiated plans and dreams for that community and then bringing people along. The vision should be so powerful that any halfway spiritual believer can grasp its significance and any gossip raised against it will seem foolish.

Credible Character: Paul knew that the enemy would use every weapon in his arsenal against him and the kingdom. He anticipated the persecution of gossip but reminded believers of how to minimize its effect.

> *"Who is there to harm you if you prove zealous for what is good? ...keep a good conscience so that in the thing in which you are slandered, those who revile your good behavior in Christ will be put to shame" (1 Peter 3:13, 15).*

The great cowboy theologian, Will Rogers, said you should, "Live in such a way that you would not be ashamed to sell your parrot to the town gossip!" When our behavior is above reproach and our conscience is clean, we starve wildfire.

God says that unwarranted gossip cannot ultimately destroy us. "Like a sparrow in its flitting, like a swallow in its flying, so a curse without cause will not alight" (Proverbs 26:2).

Although people may still gossip, a leader who is above reproach in his character will not fall. In fact, a gossip will always be exposed in the end for what they really are.

This also means that we do not place gossips in positions of influence or leadership. Why would we give a known slanderer a greater platform to destroy the church? As shepherds we are responsible to guard the flock from wolves in sheep's clothing. It will cause problems, but a gossip that is in a position of authority must be dealt with and if unrepentant, ultimately removed. You can anticipate some trouble when you approach this because this is just one more opportunity for them to do what they do best. But it must be done or the cancer will remain and grow.

Paul is so adamant about this that he even extends it to the benevolence ministry of the church. In the New Testament, the church took care of their widows. But not all of them. Those who had children were to be taken care of by their own family as the children "gave some return" to their parents. And a widow who was a gossip or busybody was not to be put on the list (1 Timothy 5:13). Gossip disallows the blessings and benefits of God.

Clear Standards: One of the greatest means of controlling gossip is to deal with it at the point of membership in the church. I once heard Jim Cymbala, pastor of Brooklyn Tabernacle in New York, share how he warns every new member about gossip as they join the church.

At the church I pastor, we have done the same in our membership process since its inception. We explain why gossip is so deadly because it can destroy the unity of the church and the picture of God to a watching world. We are seeking to develop a community filled with love, and gossip treats others like dirt.

I relay to them that we are "death on gossip" and that if they ever hear me speaking of someone in an unbiblical manner, they have the right and responsibility to come to me about it. And our leaders will do the same with them. It's interesting to observe that genuine believers greatly appreciate this approach and it eliminates gossip. I know that the potential is always there, but for the last decade we have had the joy of living in a church with little gossip and slander. It is one of the great keys, I believe, to growth and accelerating a right opinion of God in a community.

But what do you do if the train has already left the station? How do you deal with wildfire that has begun to spread in your church? What reactive steps must be taken if gossip is present?

Speed: You don't wait to combat wildfire as it races through a forest. Firefighters must be mobilized immediately or it will merely accelerate the destruction. When church leaders hear of gossip they must not just talk about it, but begin steps to quench it quickly.

Verification: Gossip by its very nature is usually untruthful. If it's not, it usually becomes so as it filters through various voices and interpretations. Just like the old game of "Gossip"…repeat a sentence often enough and by the time it gets around the circle it will bear no semblance to its original statement. If you hear gossip, you need to seek to verify what has really been said.

Privacy: Just as Matthew, Chapter 18 says, when we hear of sin or experience it, we should go and confront the individual in question privately. Often it is a misunderstanding. If not, it brings the issue into the open where it can be dealt with in grace and truth. If an individual is committing the sin of gossip and is unwilling to deal with it, the further steps of Matthew 18 must be taken.

There is a special injunction given by God to protect His church against people who are spreading strife and division in the church in Titus 3:10-11:

> *"Reject a factious man after a first and second warning, knowing that such a man is perverted and is sinning, being self-condemned."*

I believe this refers to a person who, after observation, is factious at the core. They must be dealt with even more quickly than others because anything and everything you do with them will just create more division. A factious man doesn't care. He will just become more factious when confronted. He loves to draw a crowd and doesn't care who it affects or how badly it ruins the reputation of Christ in a community. Steps of church discipline including the exclusion of membership should be taken, Paul says, after a second and third warning.

Further, there may be multiple people involved in this sin. They should all be dealt with privately if possible. There may be a case where the gossip is so prevalent it must be dealt with corporately. But caution must be taken that a church leader doesn't take out his shotgun and blast away at the entire congregation, leveling innocent bystanders in the process.

And there's one more caution given in Scripture and it deals with accusations and gossip against church leaders. Leaders are always vulnerable to what everyone thinks or says about them. They can be accused, tried, convicted, and executed right in the hallways of the church! Therefore, Paul gives this statement about dealing with church leaders:

> *"Do not receive an accusation against an elder except on the basis of two or three witnesses" (1 Timothy 5:19).*

This doesn't mean that sinning leaders shouldn't be held accountable. It does imply that we need to move with caution. If a leader is found in some sin that is harming the flock and aborting his leadership, he bears a greater responsibility than the normal believer. With leadership comes responsibility. The judgment upon sinning leaders is significant because their lives affect so many others. Paul instructs that "those who continue in sin" we should "rebuke in the presence of all so that the rest also will be fearful of sinning" (1 Timothy 5:20).

Reconciliation: The great goal of church discipline is the reputation of God, the purity of the church, and the restoration of the individual. The purpose of confronting gossip is contained in these three statements. If a believer has been gossiping and is found guilty and repents, encourage them to go to everyone they have spoken to and seek their forgiveness and the clearing of their conscience. This could spread like wildfire too and has even been used of God to bring great revival to churches in the past.

One final note on this important topic. If you are put in the position where you must deal with gossip, be careful that you do not commit the same sin! If you are seeking to verify and rectify gossip, there may have to be some discussions with others to get to the root of the issue. But it is very tempting to go beyond genuine steps of reconciliation, particularly if the gossip has your name on it. Gossip is about revenge. It is a tool to hurt people who have hurt you. Don't stoop to the same sinful responses that have so brutally affected your own reputation.

> *"Let no unwholesome (literally "rotten") word come out of your mouth, but only such a word as is good for edification according to the need of the moment so that it will give grace to those who hear. Do not grieve the Holy Spirit by whom you were sealed for the day of redemption. Let all bitterness and wrath and anger and clamor and slander be put away from you along with all malice. Be kind to one another, tender-hearted, forgiving each other just as God in Christ also has forgiven you" (Ephesians 4:29-32).*

Seasons of gossip are very revealing. Mark Twain said, "If you hold a cat by the tail you learn things you can't learn any other way." God occasionally puts us in places we never planned to visit, but there's much to be learned on the journey. Even gossip, when dealt with God's way, will show you things about yourself, others, God, and His church that will help you and your whole church in the future.

Navigation Gate #8:

- Make a list of any specific ways gossip has invaded your church right now and determine with your leadership team the next steps to deal with it. Be careful to ruthlessly evaluate your own sins in this area as well.

From: Matt Johnson
To: Jim Bradford
CC:
Subject: Hurt

Dear Jim,

Thanks so much for all your great counsel. I can't express how much it's helped me. And I guess that's why I'm writing you again.

I've got something going on in me that I've never experienced. I guess I've never been through quite this much personal attack and it keeps coming. But I'm finding myself really upset…a lot. I can't seem to get past what people are doing to me, my family, and God's church. I know I probably shouldn't be so thin-skinned, but this is just about the most painful thing I've ever been through.

I've preached on forgiveness before, and experienced it. But I'm finding it very hard to release those who've done so much damage. I'd love your thoughts on this. I feel like I'm drowning in my own bitterness.

Thanks,

Matt

- -

From: Jim Bradford
To: Matt Johnson
CC:
Subject: RE: Hurt

Dear Matt,

If you'd never written your last email I would have wondered if you were a human being! The magnitude of what you're going through and the personal nature of some of the attacks is great fuel for unforgiveness.

Everybody gets hurt, Matt, in one way or another. Church leaders can couch this in spiritual terms, but in reality it's not the hurt that's the problem—it's how I deal with hurt that is the issue. This conflict you're experiencing will either make you better or bitter. The ash heap of ministry is covered with the remains of many men who never understood this and carried bitterness till their death.

I've had to learn these lessons the hard way. I wouldn't choose those seasons, but I wouldn't trade them for anything either. Really understanding forgiveness on the anvil of pain has been the most important lesson of my life.

Praying for you,

Jim

CHAPTER NINE

Forgiving Enemies

"How do I handle the hurt?"

We sat across a light lunch in his office. Jim White was with the Navigator ministry staff and had become my dear friend, confidant, and spiritual counselor. It seems we had lunch just about every time I found myself drowning. We were in the midst of a major conflict over the direction of the church, which was to be my first big leadership challenge.

Today was the worst. The center of the storm for me had a face. My antagonist at the church was one of the most bitter men I had ever encountered. His bitterness was couched in spirituality as he had controlled the church for years. And now his attack had turned on me. I was young, overwhelmed, hurt, and had no idea what to do. "What am I going to do about this man?" I asked Jim.

After I'd poured out my soul, Jim did what he always did. He turned in his Bible to Romans 12:17-21, but he didn't need to, for he had memorized this passage long ago:

> *"Never pay back evil for evil to anyone. Respect what is right in the sight of all men. If possible, as far as it lies within you, be at peace with all men. Never take your own revenge, beloved, but leave room for the wrath of God, for it is written, 'Vengeance is mine, I will repay,' says the Lord. But if your enemy is hungry, feed him and if he is thirsty, give him a drink. For in so doing you will heap burning coals on his head. Do not be overcome by evil, but overcome evil with good."*

He closed his Bible and made a statement that I'll never forget. "God only allows two people in the boxing ring at once, Bill," he said. "If you want Him to fight your battle, you must get out of the ring."

This period in my ministry began a series of experiences in which God taught me one of the most vital lessons of life. If you are going to make it in service to God and others, you must learn how to forgive. There is no other option.

Have you ever been hurt?

Kind of a dumb question, isn't it? Life is full of hurts and all you have to do is breathe to experience pain. It may have been in your past with family, friends, or enemies. Or maybe you're experiencing some real hurt right now. We all go through problems and pain. The question is not "Have you been hurt?" but "How have you handled the hurts of your heart?"

Believe it or not, harbored hurt has the same root as all other sins. It is centered in our pride. We believe we deserve certain things in life. I've often said that we really don't want to get into a discussion with God about what we deserve! But out of this sense of entitlement we form certain expectations.

"I expect people to like me and treat me well."

"I expect good health."

"I expect a husband/wife who will always honor and respect me."

"I expect to go into ministry and have every church member really treat me well."

"I expect that every professing believer would naturally want the things God wants."

"I expect to be successful."

"I expect that, if I'm leading fairly well, people will follow my leadership."

There is nothing wrong with a passion and burden for good things to happen. But the reality of living in a sin-wrecked world means that all of our expectations in life are never met. When we fail to see some of our dreams met we get hurt. And when hurt has a face on it we can harbor that pain and hold something in our heart against them. Held long enough this turns into a root of bitterness, which God says will always spring up, always cause trouble, and always affects those around us (Hebrews 12:15).

Harbored hurt always manifests itself. When we have been hurt we develop strategies to avoid this pain in the future. Anger, a quick temper, oversensitivity, withdrawal, fear, the inability to trust—they are all merely strategies we have consciously or unconsciously developed to avoid pain in the future.

Conflict in the church can get messy. Church leaders can overcome a lot of mistakes, but there's one error that is deadly. In the midst of the conflict you must forgive! If not, you run the risk of picking up the disease of bitterness which will consume you the rest of your life in ways you will not recognize and cannot imagine.

How in the world do I forgive?

Forgiveness is a grace-empowered choice of the will to release a debt, by faith, for the glory of God.

"I can't forgive. You don't realize what they did to me." Satan loves to make us believe we are the only ones who have been hurt like this. But the reality is there is no "trial overtaken you but such as is common to man" (1 Corinthians 10:13).

Others have gone through what you've experienced and worse and still found God's grace to forgive. Forgiveness is not an act of your emotions, it a choice and one that many others have made.

If you had done some work on my house for me and I owed you money, you could forgive that debt if you desired. It's not a step of your emotions, it's a choice of your will. You can forgive anybody. In fact, God cannot by His very nature ask you to do something that you can't do by His grace. And He says, "forgive, just as I have forgiven you" (Matthew 6:14; Ephesians 4:32).

I often ask people who are wrestling with this issue to sit down and make a list of all the hurts they've experienced in life. If they will honestly do this exercise they are always surprised at the amount of hurt they are carrying in the ledger book of their heart. When Paul is describing for us what the love of God is all about he uses an accounting term. "Love…does not take into account a wrong suffered" (1 Corinthians 13:5). He doesn't write it down.

The only reason we mentally and emotionally record what others have done is so we can exact payment. They owe us. We want revenge. We may not even understand this and surely wouldn't verbalize it, but we want them to hurt like we have. We want them to pay for what they've done ("It's not fair!") and we are amazingly creative in our means of exacting payment. We can gossip. This tears them down before others. We can withdraw and not speak to them, thinking this will cause them pain. We can go on the attack to thwart their plans, just as we feel they have aborted ours. We can explode in anger or implode in depression. And on and on. We're good at this.

Forgiveness releases the debt. It strikes it off the ledger book of our heart. "They owe me nothing. I chose to forgive and release them from their debt," is a statement I have said out loud thousands of times.

"But what they did was wrong. If I forgive them, who will take care of correcting this?"

Forgiveness is a choice of my will…by faith. Jim White reminded me that pivotal day that forgiveness doesn't let people off the hook. It just transfers the issue from my courtroom into the courtroom of heaven. "Vengeance is mine, I will repay," says the Lord. "Leave room for the wrath of God." God is extremely capable of taking care of others and adjusting accounts as needed. I can trust Him. My job is to forgive and leave the results to Him.

It is important to note that some issues may still need to be addressed biblically. But if you have not truly forgiven, you will approach this confrontation with a subtle desire for revenge. Only when you take the "log" of unforgiveness out of your eye are you able to help your brother with the "speck" in his eye. If you've ever had a speck of anything in your eye you know that you want it removed. And, you also know that you want someone who sees well to be doing the removing! Forgiveness puts us in the position to genuinely help others.

"I don't think I have the ability to forgive them," you might say. And you would be accurate. Forgiveness is a choice of my will made possible by the grace of God. There is much in this life that I'm incapable of doing. That's why I need God and His amazing, enabling, sufficient grace. And there's one pathway to receive grace.

"God resists the proud, but gives grace to the humble" (James 4:6).

Humility is the willingness to admit my sin and acknowledge my need. As soon as I take that step, the grace of God pours from heaven because God loves to manifest His power through our weakness. This moment of hurt is one of the greatest opportunities you will ever have to experience God. You need HIM. You must cry out for grace, admitting your inability to forgive, and trust in His empowering grace.

You're never more like Jesus than when you forgive.

Every church leader knows he must be an example to those around him if he is to be effective. We are to forgive for the glory of God. We desire to magnify Him, to give the world a right opinion of the God we know and serve. And He is a forgiving God. If you have any trouble believing this, sit down and start writing out a list of all the sins you've ever committed!

"Be kind to one another, tender-hearted, forgiving each other just as God in Christ has forgiven you" (Ephesians 4:32), is not a suggestion. It is a reminder that God has been extremely patient with us and we need to extend that grace to those who've hurt us.

It is the primary conduit for us to release the love of God through our lives to others and a watching world.

The greatest evidence of God is His love flowing through you against the backdrop of hurt. The endgame of forgiveness is not a little relief for you or for others. It is to clear your heart of all that would abort the love of God so His Divine compassion can flow through you to others. When that love is seen, God is seen… and glorified.

So I chose to forgive. Leaving Jim's office, I went off to a retreat center that I often used for study and meditation and met with God. I took out a sheet of paper and began to list all the ways I had been hurt. I was shocked at its length. When I felt that the Spirit had taken me everywhere He desired to go, I began to go back over that black list of hurts. One-by-one I struck a line through each and verbalized this prayer to my forgiving Father: "Lord, I choose to forgive this. Thank you for your grace. And thank you for allowing this to come into my life so I can experience the empowering grace of Your forgiveness flowing through me."

As I finished that list, I sensed an amazing liberty. I was free! What could man do to me? God would take care of any issues necessary. I had transferred everyone (even my bitter enemy) to God's courtroom.

And then I realized there was one more step. "Lord, shed abroad your love in my heart by the Holy Spirit" (Romans 5:5). "You live in me, and you are love. All the love I need is present in me. I give you my arms and eyes and legs and body to be used as instruments of righteousness" (Romans 6:13). I asked Him to let His love, which is a fruit of the Spirit, flow through me like "rivers of living water" (Galatians 5:22; John 7:37-39).

You may not believe this, but the next time I saw that old, bitter man who'd hurt me, I loved him. And I've loved him ever since. I didn't like or approve of what he was doing. In fact, his divisiveness became so problematic that our leadership team had to take the necessary steps to deal with him for the sake of the church.

But I was able to continually respond to him with forgiveness and love. Each time I started to pick up that unforgiveness again I would quickly choose to forgive and strike it from the ledger. I wanted to keep short accounts.

Once, years later, he called a church that was approaching me to be their pastor and slandered me to try to keep me from getting the job. That old feeling of anger began to well up in my heart. It was now time to deal with one final test of forgiveness. God takes us through moments like this when we're ready, peeling off layer after layer of our harbored hurts. I entertained the idea of starting my own telephone campaign, but quickly realized the folly of taking my own revenge. I chose (again) to forgive and asked for God's love to flood my heart. The response God gave me was to send him an anonymous gift with a note telling him that I loved him.

The only explanation for forgiveness is God. You can forgive—and even love—your enemies because the God of love lives in you. And you never look more like Him than when you forgive.

Navigation Gate #9:

- Write down a list of anything or anyone that has hurt you. Be completely honest and thorough. One-by-one, walk through each item and pray a prayer of forgiveness and then mark through those issues, transferring them to God's courtroom. Clear your conscience with anyone necessary and then determine to keep short accounts.

  (For further study, order our booklets, *Forgiveness: Healing the Harbored Hurts of your Heart* and *Lifting Life's Greatest Load: How to Gain and Maintain a Clear Conscience.*)

From: Matt Johnson
To: Jim Bradford
CC:
Subject: family

Dear Jim,

I thought we'd hit bottom. But a few nights ago I got a blow I wasn't expecting. One of my four kids came into our room and poured out her heart. She'd overheard some adults talking at church about me in a derogatory way. "Daddy, why do these people hate you?"

I can take a lot, but I don't think I can handle my kids and wife suffering through this. Maybe it's time for me to leave.

Discouraged,

Matt

- -

From: Jim Bradford
To: Matt Johnson
CC:
Subject: RE: family

Dear Matt,

There's nothing more painful than seeing your family hurt. When the sin of others affects them, something rises up in us as parents—a defense response—that overpowers almost every other natural instinct.

And we should protect them. The important thing is to do it God's way. To fail to find Him here and use His processes to protect your family could have tragic effects for your wife and kids.

The reality is that we will never be able to distance our children from every hurt in life. That is why we must walk through these experiences with them and help them see it all through God's eyes. The same grace you need is the grace and perspective they need.

I've been through it, and believe it or not my family grew through the experience. It's possible and I'm enclosing some further thoughts that might help you find God's path to REAL protection for your family.

By God's grace,

Jim

CHAPTER TEN

PROTECTING FAMILY
"How do I help those I love the most?"

"Friendly fire" is a contradictory statement. It's the term used in warfare describing the tragedy of combatants hitting their own troops. No one intends for this to happen, and aggressive preparation is made to try and prevent it, but it still occurs.

A recent study by "Intimate Encounters" indicated that 80% of pastors believe pastoral ministry is negatively affecting their families. Many pastors have lost their first church (their families) on the altar of their ministry. Teenagers who see the hypocrisy and sinfulness of church conflict can become tremendously disillusioned, giving great ground for the enemy's temptations to walk away from the church…and often from the Lord.

As we've said, church conflict is not an intrusion to pastoring, it is pastoring. If God has called you to a place of service, He has called your wife and children too and He is very aware of the environment He's placing them in. God knows the way for this spot to become a place of training, growth, and victorious service for them just as it is for you. If handled properly, seasons of conflict can be some of the hardest, but most beneficial moments of their spiritual lives.

Protecting Your Wife

When a pastor or church leader is under attack in the midst of conflict, it is very easy for the wife to take up an offense on his behalf. She should defend her husband. But if that defense leads to unforgiveness, a root of bitterness and cynicism can grow in her heart for years—even past the initial conflict. How can this be avoided? How can we be of the greatest help to our wives in times of difficulty in the church?

Let her in. Often, as church leaders, we find ourselves so overwhelmed with the issues and pain surrounding church conflict that we withdraw. We may have talked about the issues all day at the office and when we come home we want to sit down and not talk. And, some pastors have been erroneously taught not to communicate with their wives about "church matters" thinking they should always spare them from the gory details of ministry.

A church leader's wife is his partner in ministry. They are one. If he does not communicate well he runs the risk of letting her come to her own conclusions without the context he has. Your wife knows you better than anyone. If you are silent she realizes something is wrong but may believe it is all about your relationship—that the conflict you're having is with her. This misunderstanding can cause relational problems in the home, which is the last thing that should happen, particularly in a time of conflict. Husband and wife need to be united and the only way that can happen is good communication.

Be honest. Don't sugarcoat or spiritualize your pain. If you are hurting, tell her. If you're upset, let her bear your burden "and thus fulfill the law of Christ" (the law of love as seen in Galatians 6:1-3). She is your helpmate and will find some of her greatest fulfillment in helping her husband in just such a time. Never underestimate the ability of God's grace to help her understand and see things you may never notice. If you hide the real issues you both will miss these vital components.

Allow her time. Your mate will stand one day before God by herself. This ministry conflict is a part of her life and spiritual growth just as much as it is yours. Allow your wife the same patience and understanding that you desire as she wrestles through the emotional impact of conflict. There will be moments she needs to process out loud, just like you. Don't give her pat biblical answers or patronizing statements when you realize she needs to "let go" and work it through out loud. Give her the same grace you desire.

Find God together. When we dump a burden on our mate they carry it too. The next step should be to find God together through His word and prayer. We hold the burden before our mate so they can engage in its weight with us. But then we must take it to the Lord and discharge it before Him in prayer. We "cast all our care upon the Lord" and together find God (1 Peter 5:7). You should lead her there.

If your mate never sees you finding God it will be hard for her to do the same. Your example of faith in God's sufficiency is vital for her to see. You may scratch and crawl your way to God, but you must get there nonetheless.

Listen. Your wife may be one of the primary tools God uses to speak to you. Don't marginalize her by saying, "You just don't understand," or "That will never work," as she seeks to give you counsel. You will disagree at times about what to do, but give her grace and listen carefully. You will find that she knows you and is mightily equipped by God to meet your needs. There is a spiritual grace and power given by God to her to fulfill her God-given role in your life…and that includes counsel in times of conflict.

Give thanks. It is easy to share the burdens and forget to tell her about the victories that occur. We all need to hear what God is doing and one of the best ways is to praise the Lord continually. God said, "In everything give thanks for this is the will of God in Christ Jesus for you" (1 Thessalonians 5:18).

Regular thanksgiving reminds both you and your wife that God is sovereign and there is nothing beyond His reach. There is always something to give thanks for.

Thank Him for what He's teaching you. Thank Him for those in the church who are standing with you. Thank Him that He knows what He's doing and has not abandoned you. The list is endless and our gratitude should be also. Notice that the Psalms David wrote alternate between pleas for mercy and help with his enemies and praise to God for His sufficiency. Life is a mixed bag, but there is always something for which to thank God. A good church leader should consistently model thanksgiving before his wife and family.

Don't misdirect frustration. Friendly fire can come from a hurting husband as well as a hypocritical church member. People who are hurt, hurt others. It is imperative that you understand the source of your frustrations and not come home and unload your anger on your family. They will not be able to distinguish the source of your irritation and they are not your enemies. Be godly enough to make the distinction and deal with it yourself.

Retreat. You need periodic retreats with your wife. A weekly date is an important getaway for her as well as you. In times of conflict it may not be possible or wise for an extended time away, but short day trips or one-night escapes will also help relieve the pressure valve. An occasional diversion is like an oasis in the desert and can prepare you for the next leg of the journey.

Most importantly, you must realize that your wife is with you in every stage of church life. She is there to share the victories, but also the sorrows. It is her life and ministry as well. Her security is deeply tied to the willingness of her husband to let her in, let her do what she is gifted to do, and for both of you to find God in the midst of the battles that rage. Without this unity the two of you are not able to do the next most important thing in your home.

Protecting your Children

I've been through two grueling church battles and various skirmishes. I also have eight children. We've had kids in every age group in the church from bed babies to college students (and now beyond!) through all of this. By the grace of God, our kids all have a passion for ministry and think it is a noble task and a high calling. In fact, they are all engaged in ministry in some form or another. They love the church and believe the greatest thing in life they can do is live for the advancement of God's kingdom. I say this not to brag, but to illustrate my belief that it is possible to take your kids through church conflict and come out healthy.

I've known many men who have left the ministry completely because they believed it was too costly for their children. I can understand this logic, but I don't agree with it. Is there a way to make church conflict a time of spiritual development for our kids? To help them instead of hurt them?

Age appropriate disclosure. Corrie ten Boom was once standing on a train platform with her father and asked him a question about sex. He determined that it was a little too soon for him to answer the particular question she was asking. He asked her to pick up his big suitcase beside him. She gave it a valiant attempt but couldn't lift it. He said, "Corrie, there are some things that are just a little too heavy for children to handle. When you get to an age where I believe you can carry that answer well, I'll tell you everything you want to know."

Our children don't need to know everything about the conflicts we face in the church. Only God can help you with the particulars of this, but they should certainly not know personalities. They should never hear the "gossip details." We should never vent in frustration before our children. And there are things that a teenager can handle that a nine-year-old cannot. I must be wise in giving them what the Lord directs and what I believe, as their parent, is something they can carry spiritually.

Biblical context. As a church leader I must find God and His direction in the midst of any conflict. When my children begin to ask me questions, or there are issues I know they are going to observe or hear, I need to couch that in the proper biblical context.

I can show my kids in the scripture where God speaks about "tares sown among the wheat" and the behavior of lost church members. I can help them see the role of church leaders to guard and protect the flock. I can also show them the passages and model myself what forgiveness is all about and the balance of truth and grace. I need to give them biblical context. In this light, issues make sense.

Don't vent. There are times in conflict when a leader needs someone who will just listen as he "blows off steam" or processes his frustration out loud. He also needs to come back to find God's perspective after this happens. But, this should NEVER happen before our children. If we are angry and our children see anger's manifestations, our wrong responses become their excuse for the same behavior. You may vent, then go find God. They may get angry, taking up an offense on your behalf and never be able to overcome it.

Stand. A biblical conviction is not something you hold, it is something that holds you. Real leaders have deep convictions. They carry the leader through the confusing fog of conflict. You must live and move out of these convictions but in times of conflict these convictions are deeply tested. A leader's children need to see their father standing for what is right. Not standing merely to defend Himself or for personal gain, but taking a biblical position and not moving.

Faith. Everything is about faith. God is constantly allowing us all to go through circumstances that are designed to take us from independence to dependence. This is true about your children as well as you. This is a faith moment for them. Help them see this and help them find God, His promises in His word, His enduring and comforting presence. God can use conflict, properly managed, in your children to mature their faith if you'll help them there.

Understand. Just as this is hard for you, it is difficult for your children. You must always be very intentional about talking to your children, but especially in times of church conflict. You must never brush aside an honest question or fail to engage. These are the formative learning moments of their lives. They need to understand the value of the kingdom, the role of the church, the responsibilities of church leaders, the nature of sin, the beauty and importance of forgiveness, as well as the balance of grace and truth. All these lessons and more can be learned during seasons of conflict if you take the time to talk with your kids. If you fail to have these necessary conversations, they may slide into wrong ideas that affect them for years.

Times of conflict come in everyone's life. One of our jobs as parents is to prepare our children for these. Training comes by teaching and on-the-job experience. Although you might not choose this moment or this way to train your children, God in His sovereignty has allowed it. Therefore, it can "work together for good" for both you and your children to "conform you (and them) to the image of God's son" (Romans 8:28-29, added parenthesis).

Remember that your children will take their cues from you. Your frustration can be their excuse for anger. If you become bitter, it will open the door for them. If you gossip they will feel vindicated as they talk about others.

Conversely, your forgiveness is an undeniable example to them. Your graciousness brings grace to them. Your stand on biblical truth shows them its value. What a treasure for a child to be able to say later in life, "Life has its conflicts. My mom and dad faced some huge issues in the church before. But I watched them respond with courageous convictions, humble forgiveness, and amazing love. If they did that then, by the grace of God, I can walk through the issues I'm facing now."

There have been millions of children in history who have watched their believing parents in times of conflict and suffering. Some have even watched their fathers burned at the stake for their convictions. You are not alone in this mighty battle that has waged for centuries between God and Satan for the souls of men. Leave your children a legacy they will never forget.

NAVIGATION GATE #10:

- Read through this chapter aloud with your wife. Engage in an honest discussion of how you are both doing in this area. Identify what you can do better to help each other and help your children.
- If you know that your children have already been adversely affected by your wrong responses, take some time to confess this to them and ask their forgiveness. Help them see the value of conflict and how God can use it in each of their lives if properly handled.

From: Matt Johnson
To: Jim Bradford
CC:
Subject: the elephant in the room

Dear Jim,

Well, it happened. I finally had someone ask me how long I thought I'd be here at the church. Their brashness about it kinda' blew me away. But the reality is, I've been thinking about it.

Jim, I'm worn out. I've been fighting this battle for a long time and the last 18 months have been really intense. Every time I think I see a light at the end of the tunnel I realize it's a train coming my way! And I seem to disappoint everybody. My family is getting the "dregs" of my life. I wonder if my leaders believe fully in me anymore. And then there are those who are actively opposing me and the direction we're headed. I just wonder if everyone wouldn't be better off if I just moved on to another field. Maybe starting a church somewhere would be a good idea.

Just wondering,

Matt

- -

From: Jim Bradford
To: Matt Johnson
CC:
Subject: RE: the elephant in the room

Dear Matt,

I'm surprised we haven't had this conversation sooner! I want you to know that it is natural to have these thoughts. Even the Apostle Paul longed to be released from the burdens of ministry and life and looked forward to the escape of heaven (Philippians 1:23-26). Thousands of pastors leave their churches every year. The great tragedy is that some do not move by God's initiation.

If you leave, you need to make sure it is God releasing you and calling you somewhere else. Without that sense of His leadership you will always wonder. Take a minute and read through the enclosure I'm sending. It'll be worth your time and could spare you from a rash mistake.

I'm praying for you,

Jim

CHAPTER ELEVEN

Moving On

"How is this going to end?"

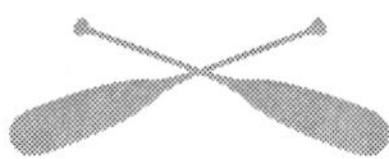

Pastors don't stay long in most churches. The average tenure for pastors in America is 2-4 years. Studies also indicate that the most productive years of ministry for a church leader in most churches is during year five through 15. It's easy to see why both pastors and churches are not developing successfully.

Not only are pastors leaving churches, they're leaving the ministry altogether at a record pace. Some denominations are even reporting a serious shortage of available pastors. Recent studies from the Fuller Institute for Church Growth and Evangelism, The Barna Group, and Pastoral Care, Inc. indicate the following:

- 90% of the pastors studied feel they are inadequately trained to cope with their ministry responsibilities.
- 50% feel unable to meet the demands of the job.
- 70% say they have a lower self-image now than when they first started.
- 70% do not have someone they consider a close friend.
- 40% report serious conflict with a church member at least once a month.
- 50% have considered leaving the ministry in the last months.
- 50% of the ministers starting out will not last five years.

- Only one out of every ten ministers will actually retire as a minister in some form.
- More than 1,700 pastors left the ministry every month last year.

Leading a church is hard. If you took the components of a pastor's task and put them in a secular job ad it might read like this:

- "Must be able to lead a volunteer organization of over 500 people. Responsible for the development and administration of a $1 million annual budget and staff of ten. Oversee maintenance of facilities and financial administration.
- Responsible to communicate powerful, 30-minute messages one to three times weekly. Administrate five different divisions representing multiple age groups and interests. Coordinate cooperation and interaction with national entities.
- Must mobilize people in effective overseas operations as well as local and national connections. Personal counseling for four to five individuals, couples, or families with major dysfunctions weekly. Lead the organization's board. Cast vision effectively for entire organization Responsible to move this organization forward even in spite of controlling interests at times and major conflict.
- Will be expected to see a five to ten percent growth rate annually. Must assure that all emotional and spiritual needs are met of all those attending and be willing to take criticism. Must be willing to do the above with little human recognition and a salary at five to ten percent below scale. "

Sounds like a great job! Pastors and church leaders don't enroll in this to make money or get recognition. Most have entered ministry with a sincere sense of call and a desire to make a difference in God's kingdom. Many have an idealized view of church life and are blindsided by conflict. It is hard for them to imagine that people are not gladly willing to follow their leadership. When conflict comes—and stays—the question of tenure always arises. Responsible church leaders find themselves dramatically torn between the desire to "tough it out" or "bolt and run."

Is it ever right to leave in the midst of conflict? The answer to this question is not simple and a blanket statement cannot be given for every situation. The answer must always be given by the Head of the church.

God knows. He is aware of every church leader's struggles and what He is seeking to accomplish in the midst of conflict. He knows when it's time to leave and time to stay. Therefore, the answer to this issue must come in communion with Him. We must hear His voice and determine His will in the normative ways we have learned to hear Him.

God calls us to serve in His church. We are not wise enough to make that decision on our own. And, we must surrender to Him the right to do with us whatever He desires.

When God calls you to Stay

Obviously the toughest decision to make is to remain in a church in the midst of difficulty and congregational conflict. Many pastors leave their churches prematurely, particularly in the face of tough, controlling factions. At least three tragedies occur when a pastor leaves before God says he should.

First, he does not develop. There are lessons learned only on the anvil of conflict. If a pastor stays in every church for only a few years until conflict occurs and suddenly feels it's "God's will for me to leave," he never develops. He doesn't become a battle-hardened warrior and is unable to handle the tougher assignments later.

Secondly, premature leaving strengthens the hands of controllers in the church. "We've run off better men than you," they smile and say. When these men and women are not biblically confronted, they become even more determined and obstinate. The next pastor faces an even greater challenge. If he leaves too early, their power grows. Soon, a high wall of control is built that no pastor feels he can scale and the church is doomed to a slow death.

Finally, the sheep do not mature. It takes time to develop the kind of relationships that lead to true discipleship. If a pastor follows several others who only lasted a few years, most church members will not commit to him or his vision. "Why should I get too involved?" they ask. "He'll leave in a year or two and a new man will come in with a whole different vision. I've heard this before and I'm not buyin' it." And…they've got a point.

There's a term used for shepherds who run at the first sign of a wolf: hirelings. Jesus used this picture to illustrate that some men see their ministry as just a job (John 10:11-18). Others see it as their life. True shepherds see conflict as part of their calling. They exist to take care of the sheep. They are willing to stay up late and get up early, to endure hardship and suffer pain to faithfully fulfill their responsibilities. A good shepherd, Jesus said, would even give his life for the sheep. And those who do receive great, eternal reward from the Master Shepherd.

Every pastor and church leader should assume that he is to stay where he is placed. If he receives an opportunity to go elsewhere, he should make sure it is God's voice calling and not the Enemy. Satan is a "liar and father of all lies" (John 8:44). God knows where you are. If He wants you to move, He is very capable of orchestrating that in a way that is godly and timely.

When God tells you to Leave

God does move people. It is obvious from Scripture, church history, and our current experience. There are times when the Word of God, the Spirit of God and godly counselors all confirm that God is calling you to another field. Sometimes this may be in the midst of conflict.

I was never more surprised. As previously mentioned, I have been in two major church conflicts (so far) in my 40+ years of ministry. In the first experience God made it extremely obvious I was to remain right where I was. This took some convincing from God! There were moments I wanted to leave and I had some opportunities to do so. Weighing those options, though, I always came to the conclusion that God desired for me to continue in that pastorate. The climax of that season of conflict was the confrontation and church discipline of a controlling man who had held the church in his grip for many years. After he left (and a group of people with him), the church began to experience a new period of growth and joy. Today, by God's grace, that church is vibrant and growing under a wonderful pastor who has called me several times to thank me for staying through the battle.

As I came to my second great leadership challenge, several years later, I assumed I was going to be asked by God to do exactly the same. This church was two distinctly different churches in one location. We were different in philosophy, passion, style—you name it. Over a period of 18 months the battle-lines were drawn even though we never intended for that to happen. I would not go into all of the details in a book, but a series of things occurred that brought me to the lowest point of my life. I first thought I was going to die, and then I was afraid I might not! Worst of all, I knew God was going to tell me to stay right where I was. I was convinced that if I did, it would be a slow funeral because the church was unwilling to take the steps necessary for health and growth.

There was a senior adult lady on our staff that was very funny. Every time you coughed around her she'd say, "That's just how granddad sounded…right before he died!" Then, with a smile she'd add, "But, of course, he lingered and suffered, lingered and suffered before he died!"

I felt, after six-and-a-half years, that I was "lingerin' and sufferin'" with no end in sight. One night I told my wife I had to get by myself and hear from God about the future. If I couldn't hear Him I was in trouble. She knew me and understood the importance of my request, and so I checked into a local hotel with nothing but my toothbrush, a bible, and notebook. I got on my face before God, crying out for him to give me direction. I began to read from where I'd finished the day before in my normal daily reading of the Word.

Within an hour the Lord had spoken very distinctly to me. The path I was to take was perfectly clear. What I was to do, and the next step I was to take, was amazingly evident. And in the midst of all of that direction the Lord gave unmistakable guidance that if the people didn't respond, I was "free to go."

I entered the pulpit the next Sunday morning with the blessing of my leadership team and staff and shared exactly what the Lord had said. I thought that it would result in revival, but halfway through my message I thought, *"I don't think we're going to see revival today!"* I presented what I and six pastors on staff felt was our responsibility to build. I also stated what was necessary, and would be required to accomplish that, and asked them to decide if that was the kind of church they desired. If not, the Lord had given me liberty to begin a new work and I would resign, bless them, and begin a new church. It was a very unusual step, one that I wouldn't counsel anyone to take without the Lord's direction, but was exactly what the Lord had clearly told me to do.

The church was a congregationally-led body and the step failed by a margin of 33 votes. I announced my resignation and two weeks later began a church. That new church has been wonderfully blessed with God's presence and power. Great growth has occurred over the last several years and it has been, without question, the greatest pastoral experience of my life.

I am absolutely convinced that if I had taken that step in the first church, it would have been disastrous and wrong. In one church, God told me to stay. In one church, God gave me liberty to leave. Both were correct steps because the decision was left, I can honestly and humbly say, entirely up to God.

George Mueller said that the first step in decision making is to come to the place where you have no will of your own. Certainly, Christ in Gethsemane gave us the greatest illustration as He cried for the cup to pass from Him, but willingly embraced whatever His Father desired. God knows exactly what we should do. It may take some spiritual surgery to get to this point of surrender, but you must—for God's sake, your sake, your family's sake, the church's sake and the kingdom's sake—make sure you are doing precisely what the Good Shepherd desires for His sheep.

What if I'm forced to leave?

"Nationwide, about one-third (34 percent) of all pastors surveyed serve a congregation who terminated their previous pastor or who were themselves forced from their last pastoral ministry, a recent survey stated. In the Southern Baptist Convention alone, according to LifeWay Christian Resources research, about 1,000 pastors will be force-terminated this year. This is a trend that has continued for nearly two and one-half decades. That's a staggering 25,000 forced pastoral terminations since the early 1980s" (David Cox, quoted by the Arkansas Baptist Newsmagazine, May 29, 2008).

Many, many pastors will face this gut-wrenching experience in their ministry life. What do you do when you are fired by a church?

Guard against bitterness. Although people may mistreat you, realize God is not the author of sin. You must learn the art of forgiveness, even for those who "despitefully use you and say all manner of things against you falsely" for Christ's name sake (Matthew 5:11). You can forgive as we outlined in a previous chapter and you must.

Don't knee-jerk. The tendency in a moment of pain such as this is to react quickly. Some men will quickly decide that ministry is not worth the risk and walk away from it altogether. Take some time if possible. There are actually a number of ministries that are designed to help pastors in just such a season. You must evaluate this properly and respond under God's direction.

Get counsel. Around you are many pastors who have experienced what you're going through. Find a trusted, godly man and let him help you walk through this experience. Just as you would go to a good doctor in a time of physical disease, take some time and let a respected soul physician help you gain perspective and healing.

Hear God. When you have been hurt there is a tendency to close your heart to the only One who has the ultimate answers. You may feel He has let you down, but He has not. Do whatever is necessary to get to Him. Wait until you hear His voice and then move accordingly.

Let your need be known. Some men are too proud to let others know of their need for the next ministry assignment. Let your need be known to those you trust and see what God provides.

Rest in the faithfulness of God. God knows where you are. He knows the needs of your family and your own soul. His grace must be sufficient in a time like this or it is not grace! He can be trusted to provide as you move in cooperation with Him.

The Psalms are so helpful to us precisely because they were written by a man in pain. He was hunted down like a dog. Falsely accused, his name was smeared and reputation tainted simply because he walked with God. The end conclusion of the Psalms is praise in a good and faithful, sovereign God. Immerse yourself in the Psalms. It will do your soul good.

Hebrews, Chapter 12 is an encouragement to us as it records the stories of the greatest men and women of the faith. Each of these suffered and God was faithful to provide everything they needed, although often not in the way they expected. We should expect suffering in a generation that is not a friend to grace, but we can also trust in the gracious and constant provision of God.

The prayer of our heart should be that which was expressed by the great missionary to Africa, David Livingstone:

Lord, send me anywhere,
only go with me.
Lay any burden on me,
only sustain me.
And sever every tie,
but the tie that binds me
to Thy service and to Thy heart.

Why do you live?

She was a feisty woman. When I first met Sandy Fawcett and her husband, Dean, I loved them. They had a lot of spunk. I was involved in a two-week meeting in their church as we all sought for God to send revival and renewal to their congregation. Sandy and Dean quickly became friends with my wife and me.

The Lord began to move greatly. In the midst of His work, Dean came to me and admitted that he had been through a long-standing affair. It had ended but he had never shared this with his wife. This dark closet had been destroying spiritual, emotional, and physical intimacy in their lives for years. Dean wouldn't open up in any dimension to his wife for fear that his sin would be exposed.

I counseled him to share it with his wife and gave him needed instructions on the process. When he did, his wife exploded as any woman would. And she refused to forgive him. This was understandable, but it went on for days and finally a dear friend of hers encouraged her to come to me for counsel.

I remember so well sitting in a small church library across the table from Sandy. Her arms were folded which was an indication of her heart's closed condition. I talked with her about the nature of men and their sexual struggles, which didn't excuse her husband but was an attempt to help her understand the "why" of his sin. No response.

I talked to her about forgiveness as an act of her will. Nothing.

I gave her the best I had for about 45 minutes and I was still talking to a stone wall. Finally, I leaned across the table and asked her a question I had never asked anyone before.

"Sandy, why do you live?"

She sat up in her chair, her eyes alert. "What do you mean?" she asked.

"Why do you live? What is your purpose in life? What do you want your life to accomplish?" I asked. I had come to know a little bit about Sandy and I anticipated the answer.

"I want my life to glorify God. I want to live for Him," she said, her lips quivering.

"Do you realize that God is giving you the greatest opportunity to magnify Him that you may ever have in your lifetime? Because you're never more like Christ than when you forgive."

She began to weep; the dam broke and I watched this precious woman come to brokenness and forgiveness in just a few minutes of time. God can accomplish miracles like this. She ran to find her husband, expressed her forgiveness, and the next chapter of their life began.

It wasn't a simplistic road for Dean and Sandy after that. They had done a lot of damage to their relationship and it took some time to bring full healing, but they were on the way. We stayed in contact through the years. I rejoiced at each conversation to hear of their progress and ministry. They were gladly willing to tell their story and because of their transparency, God began to use them with other couples. They developed a broad ministry to many hurting people.

Almost 15 years later I received a call one day from Dean. Sandy was listening on the other line.

"Bill, can you do me a favor?" Dean asked.

"Anything for you, Dean"

"I want you to watch the Oprah Winfrey Show next week…for two days in a row!" he said.

I laughed and assured Dean that Oprah was not in my normal viewing schedule.

"I know, I know," he said. "But through a strange set of circumstances Sandy and I are going to be guests on that show. Oprah is doing a show on wives who have forgiven their husbands who have been adulterous." (This was during the period when Bill Clinton had an adulterous relationship with Monica Lewinsky.)

I dutifully turned on the television the next week. Dean and Sandy were there, along with several others. I was astounded as they began to speak. Sandy gave an incredible testimony of forgiveness, stating that it was only possible because of the grace of God. Over ten million people heard those words as God was glorified on the #1 talk show in the nation!

I wonder what would have happened to Dean and Sandy if they had not made the decisions to follow God implicitly? And I marvel at how greatly God can use us, even in our imperfections and failures, when we let Him be in control.

What is church conflict about? God desires to make it about His glory and He is looking for leaders who will take His church there. Regardless of how it starts, He can compose a story that helps people, blesses His leaders, and glorifies Himself. If you will trust Him and take the next right step, you may be astounded at how He writes the final chapter.

Navigation Gate #11:

- Have an honest discussion with your wife and another discussion with a trusted friend. Tell them exactly how you're feeling about your tenure at the church and help them see any areas where you may not be thinking correctly. Determine before God to not move without His initiation.

From: Matt Johnson
To: Jim Bradford
CC:
Subject: surprised

Dear Jim,

It's been a good while since our last email. As you know per our phone call, the Lord brought us through the final stages of the conflict here. I can't thank you enough for all the counsel and encouragement. Don't know how I would have survived without it. The church has pushed through to the other side and the future looks really bright.

In light of that, this is really going to sound crazy. But now that we've come through the conflict, I have a major desire to leave. This is ridiculous because now should be the most enjoyable moment for me as God has really positioned us to move ahead. But I'm out of gas. I'm having a real hard time finding vision for the next leg of the journey.

Battle-weary,

Matt

From: Jim Bradford
To: Matt Johnson
CC:
Subject: RE: surprised

Dear Matt,

One of the biggest shocks to me came after I had gone through my first major conflict in my first church. I assumed that since we'd struggled through, my life would be filled with joy. Instead, I felt pretty empty…and it blindsided me.

You've been fighting a hard battle for a long time, Matt. Your tanks are empty and you have no idea how tired you are. It is a very, very vulnerable time and I want to make a "doctor's prescription" for you that I hope you'll take. If you don't, you may make a step that you'll later regret. Please read the enclosed carefully!

Still praying with you,

Jim

CHAPTER TWELVE

Resisting Undertow

"What happens after it's over?"

Have you ever wondered about all the rules your mother gave you? I mean, sure, she was your mom and you assumed she was perfect, but some of the prevailing "mom-isms" have little basis in fact.

"If you keep making that face it's going to stick like that!"

"If you cross your eyes, they'll be permanently crossed!"

"You'll choke on that peanut butter!"

"You can't swim for one hour after eating!"

But one piece of advice she gave you at the beach was absolutely accurate: "Don't go out there, you'll get caught in the undertow!" You may have thought undertow was some type of sea monster, but if she said it loud enough and often enough, it was sufficient to keep you close to shore.

Undertow is a strong, subsurface flow of water that returns back towards the sea from the shore. It's powerful and can pull you under if you're not careful. Undertow is real.

The first major conflict I faced as a pastor came six years into my first pastorate after seminary. The intense season of the battle lasted about 18 months, although it brewed for several years before that time. God marvelously vindicated Himself and resolved the conflict. After it was over there was an incredible new liberty and life in the church. It was exactly what we had prayed and worked for.

So why was I not enjoying it? In an amazing emotional turn of events, I found myself strangely numb. I wasn't happy, I wasn't sad. Just numb. The challenge of now taking the church into the vision we had heard from God did not seem to ignite my soul as it had done previously. As several months rolled by, I even found myself wanting to leave the church! This was the moment when I should have been most excited, yet I couldn't muster any enthusiasm.

Then something happened to me that had not occurred in the previous 15 years of ministry. I had a strange desire to do something else: to teach in a college or seminary, or be a chaplain on a college campus. I wanted to do something related to ministry, but just different.

I wasn't smart enough to diagnose what was happening in my own soul, but a wise older pastor was. In an hour-long car ride he challenged me to get away. "You're worn out, Bill," he said. "I had a similar moment in my life. I should have taken the time to get away and hear God, but I didn't and I've always wondered if the next step I took was what God desired."

Battle Weary

We need rest. God is the One who ordained morning and evening, daylight and dark, work and sleep. He even designed a Sabbath to devote one day out of each seven to rest and reflect on Him. Why would we assume that this Divine system isn't critical? The Manufacturer of our mind, soul, and body knows our limitations. It is amazing how "fearfully and wonderfully made" we are, but also how fragile we can be. God knows what happens when we violate the operating instructions in His manual!

Any major season of conflict needs a corresponding season of rest. If you fail to recognize this, you will move forward after conflict with a blissful naivete about your true emotional state that can be deadly.

Following God's prescription always brings health. There are very important benefits of some type of sabbatical season after a time of conflict—particularly if it has been a prolonged conflict.

Rejuvenation

Sinkholes can surprise you. One day you have a beautiful lawn, the next a 30-foot crater. Scientists tell us that sinkholes are caused by the removal of support beneath the surface. This can happen over a long or short period of time, a slow decay or a sudden act of nature. It can be precipitated by the collapse of a cave roof or the erosion of rock by a steady stream of water. Men can also create it as they drain land or use up the available water table, causing the water underneath the land to dry up. Suddenly, there is no support and with virtually no warning, the ground collapses.

The gradual drip of conflict can dry us up physically, emotionally and spiritually. Our tanks get low. During times of stress we run on grace and adrenaline. After the crisis subsides, the emptiness underneath can cause us to crater. We can suffer from a lot of false guilt about our spiritual emptiness when the reality may be that we deeply need some rest. We need time to refresh our underground supply or we may face a devastating ministry sinkhole.

Also, it is important to understand that when a church goes through major conflict, there are usually a lot of people who are really praying for you as their pastor or church leader. When the crisis passes, they may have a tendency to let up on their intercession on your behalf. You may feel this loss but not be aware of its origin.

Only clarity and honesty can resolve this. You need to be candid enough with your praying friends to let them know what you're experiencing and ask them to continue in their intercession for you and your family.

Reflection

It's hard to see during conflict. Often, you're scratching just to survive and all you can focus on is the next step. There are incredibly valuable lessons that God desires for us to glean from conflict—lessons that can only be fully understood through prolonged, deliberate reflection by the aid of His Spirit and His Word.

If you will take an intentional time of rest after a season of conflict and give God time, He will make sense of all that needs to be understood. During conflict, you only see the thread and shuttle whipping through each day. During rest you see the tapestry He has been creating and are surprised at its beauty and purpose.

Redefinition and Reassignment

A man once joined our staff after being in a ministry in real turmoil. He had fought for every inch of ministry ground. An interesting phenomenon occurred as he came to our church, which was a place of great liberty, opportunity, and spiritual encouragement (a complete opposite of what he had experienced for many years). He didn't know what to do.

He was not lazy. He had never been directionless, but he was almost paralyzed by his new environment. As I helped him work through this moment, we both realized that his previous world was all defined by conflict. He had learned to be a warrior. He expected people to oppose him (which had been a right assumption in his last church). An environment of opposition had shaped all his teaching, thinking, and leading.

"You've got to redefine success," I finally told him.

"What do you mean?" he asked.

"Success in your last ministry was measured by your faithfulness to stand for the truth and fight against those who opposed you. You got good at it. You did well. But now, you are no longer in that environment. You can relax with these people. They want to hear what you have to say. They are willing to follow. You don't have to fight for things, you just need to love them and lead them." This realization brought clarity and fresh direction for his ministry.

If you have been through a time of conflict, it is all you may know. It is what shaped your days and determined your steps. When that season is over, if you're not careful, you will still have on your combat, night-vision goggles and see everything through those lenses. You may keep battling when it's really time to build.

It takes time for some people to see this. A season of rest and reflection can enable you to put the past in its proper place, redefine your role for the coming season, and be prepared to move forward to your next assignment.

Sabbaticals

If you've been through conflict recently you know you're tired. I hope, as you read, you understand the need to arrange some time away. But what you may not know is how to pull this off. Although the Sabbath rest idea originated with God and is completely Biblical and spiritual, most churches are clueless about its value. "I never got a sabbatical in my work!" some grumpy old naysayer may say (a man whose very grumpiness may have been caused because he never had a sabbatical rest!).

How do you help the church see that you're not asking for a vacation, but rather a needed time of equipping for your next season of ministry?

Be honest. Many church members would be thrilled to allow their church leaders some time if they were aware of the situation. Don't whine, but be honest about your need. Particularly, let your trusted leaders know the depth of your spiritual and emotional exhaustion.

Be realistic. Don't ask for three months off if that's not appropriate. You may need a few weeks. A month is fantastic. You know your church and what would be appropriate. But you must take enough time to be able to accomplish what needs to happen. Taking only a week off when you have the responsibility of preaching the next Sunday is no sabbatical rest!

Right after the conflict has transpired may not be the best time for a sabbatical. There may be smoldering embers from the conflict that would rekindle in your absence. Let God and your leadership team lead you into a good, appropriate time for this time away, but don't put it off indefinitely.

Be open. As your leadership team works through this with you, let them tell the church what is happening and invite them to rejoice in what God has done and what the future holds. Let them explain to the church, with your help, why you're taking some time. Your people will rejoice in this and pray for you as you're gone.

Be thoughtful. You may not be the only one on your team that needs some time. Other staff members and lay leaders may need the same consideration.

Be intentional. Don't plan a sabbatical and go on a trip with your family that is filled with constant activity. A sabbatical should include great times of refreshment and recreation with your family. It should also have extremely deliberate times of reflection and study, perhaps even writing, to let God speak to your heart. You will need to explain this to your family perhaps. Give your wife the same consideration and allow her times to get alone just as you desire.

Be proactive. Our church now carries a policy to allow our senior staff an extended sabbatical every five years. Words cannot express how I look forward to this time, need this time, and use this time. I come back better. Our leaders see that this is not wasted motion.

Be persistent. Don't procrastinate. If you need some time, push until it is accomplished and don't put it off. If you fail to do this when needed or offered, you will give the church the dregs of your life! What is better for the kingdom? To keep on giving the church mere fumes of tired leadership, or to get away for a few weeks, find renewed vision, and come back and lead with passion and vitality?

Be confident. Many pastors have an exalted view of their own importance. They think that in their absence the church is going to fall completely apart. After I returned from my first sabbatical I discovered that the church was in better shape than before I left (a little disconcerting, actually!) Men had stepped up and exhibited great leadership. The people had understood my absence because it had been properly explained. Everything was better. I lost a lot of good time through unnecessary worry about the church during my first sabbatical…and it was completely unfounded.

I took the older pastor's advice. With a little trepidation I approached my leadership team several months after the battle had ended and told them what I was feeling.

"I feel like I'm in a very vulnerable position," I said. "Out of my emotional weariness I could make a dumb mistake about the future which we'd all regret."

I was shocked at their response. They'd seen the bags under my eyes, I suppose, and understood my need. Before the meeting was over they had encouraged me to go from the week-long summer camp preaching engagement I had already calendared and take an additional three-week sabbatical.

I had no idea where to go and one of the men said, "You must go to the mountains," and he quickly arranged accommodations for our family in a small A-frame cottage sitting at 10,000 feet right above Colorado Springs, Colorado.

I'm not a hiker. Give me a good book and a recliner any day. But somehow I felt the mountains contained my salvation. Each morning I took my Bible, water, and my journal and headed into the hills. Day-by-day the Lord would speak to me. When I realized how quickly you could climb a mountain if hiking straight up, I began to set my sights on a summit at the top. It would be my ultimate goal for my sabbatical.

The day came when I headed for the top. Quickly I realized I had overestimated both the length of the climb and my physical ability! I was suckin' wind with every step, heading up through thick woods. Branches were slapping me at my head and vines were grabbing my feet. I literally pulled myself up by grabbing tree after tree. I thought I would never make it. Head down, I pulled my way through one more stand of trees and suddenly I was on the summit! I hadn't realized how close I was.

The vista below me was breathtaking. I looked at Colorado Springs, about 5,500 feet below and the flat earth as it extended and curved beyond. I looked behind me and was overwhelmed with the majesty of Pike's Peak. I sang and shouted and danced a little "gospel two-step" right on top of the mountain!

After a few minutes I sat down and the gracious Spirit of God began to speak to my heart. Thoughts began tumbling into my mind and heart. I realized that, just like the climb, I had been on an uphill pull for a long time. It had been hard—harder than anything I'd ever encountered in ministry. There were brambles at every turn and I had been suckin' wind for several years. All I had been able to see was the next step.

But there was a mountaintop. By God's grace, He had given me the strength and courage to keep going. We were making more progress than I realized. He had brought me through, and there was a destination He had planned for me and our church that was breathtaking. That encounter with the Lord of creation on His mountain restored my soul.

We were leaving the mountain the last day of our sabbatical to head home. It was a Sunday morning and I turned on the radio and some Christian music was playing. Songs from my childhood, actually. I began to sing and then an uncontrollable flood of tears came. My wife said, "Honey, why are you crying?"

I simply replied, "God has given me back my song."

Navigation gate #12

...the finish line!

- If you have come through church conflict, ask your leaders for some time away. Spend this time productively as outlined in this chapter. Make a record during this time of everything God has taught you in this season and share it with your wife and then with your leaders as you return.

THE DIVINE CONJUNCTION

God's grace intersects our lives to bring change that would be impossible without Him. "I am what I am," Paul admitted, "by the grace of God." God's initiating intervention gives us something we could not have, makes us something we would not be, and uses us to bless others in ways we could never dream.

The Bible describes grace often with two simply words: **"but God."** Simple men and women are made heroes in God's story not by their mighty works, but because of this Divine conjunction.

Noah, as he was used to save the human race, when surrounded by the flood:

> *"And the water prevailed over the whole earth...* ***but God****... remembered Noah and his family" (Genesis 7:24-8:1).*

Abraham, as he became the father of the nation through whom all the world would be blessed, when tempted to intervene:

> *"And Abraham said to God, 'Oh that Ishmael might live before You!'...* ***but God*** *said, "No, but Sarah your wife will bear you a son, Isaac...and I will establish My covenant with him for an everlasting covenant (Gen 17:18-19).*

Joseph, as he was placed—through his brothers' ill treatment—in a position to save the entire world:

> *"As for you, you meant evil against me,* ***but God*** *meant it for good in order to bring about this present result, to preserve many people alive (Genesis 50:20).*

David, as he waited in hiding to take his place as Israel's greatest king:

"My flesh and my heart may fail, **but God** *is the strength of my heart and my portion forever (Psalm 73:26).*

Paul, as he brought the gospel to the Gentiles:

"...we were afflicted on every side: conflicts without, fears within, **but God,** *who comforts the depressed, comforted us..." (2 Corinthians 7:5-6).*

Even Christ Himself, in His role as a man dying in our place, receives this Divine intervention of grace:

"godless men...put Him to death, **but God** *raised Him up again..." (Acts 2:23-25).*

And there is a Divine conjunction in your story if you have tasted already of God's grace:

"And you were dead in your trespasses and sin... **but God** *...made you alive together with Christ" (Ephesians 2:1-5).*

It is important to understand that each of these men was prepared for grace by difficulty, pain, and need. These necessary moments brought them to the end of their resources. There was nothing they could do to save themselves and God became the hero.

We must not misinterpret grace. Grace comes not only in the rescue, but also in the preparation. Paul saw this so clearly that he began to "glory in his weakness" for he knew it was setting him up for God's power to be manifested through greater grace.

Do not resist difficulty and do not misunderstand its intent. The Divine conjunction always results in purposes beyond our imagination. Excruciating moments of need followed by exquisite grace make us a pathway of blessing to others. "The stewardship of God's grace was given to me for you," Paul wisely said. Who could dream that our need, interrupted by God's grace, could lead to such usefulness, service, and joy?

"But God."

APPENDIX A

50 Marks of a Man of God

Personal Questions From
The pastoral epistles for men
In christian leadership

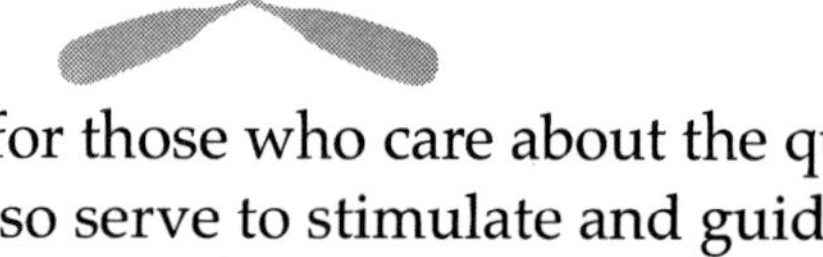

These questions are for those who care about the quality of their leadership. They also serve to stimulate and guide aspiring leaders (1Timothy 3:1). There is nothing light or empty here. Only serious men will proceed and gain from the exercise of facing biblical evaluation. Will you treat these questions with the respect, concern, and humility that they deserve? Your leadership may depend on it.

The Pastoral epistles confront apathy, moral compromise, and lack of decisiveness often found in Christian leadership. Instruction is given to elders, deacons, and missionaries (e.g. Timothy and Titus) as to how they are to live as examples – examples for all believing men to follow.

Use your heart and your pen to evaluate. Write out your thoughts in the margin. Contemplate. Pray. Above all, be honest.

ᘓ

1 Timothy 3

1. Are you above reproach? Blameless in every area of life? Do you have a good reputation with those inside and outside the church? (v. 2, 7)

☐ Yes ☐ No

2. Are you a one-woman man? Do you have a single-minded devotion to your wife? Are you overcoming problems of lust and moral impurity? (v. 2)

☐ Yes ☐ No

3. Are you temperate, sober, and serious-minded about the things of God? Are you vigilant and watchful about your personal life? (v. 2)

☐ Yes ☐ No

4. Are you prudent and sensible? Do you exhibit common sense regarding the basic issues of your life and ministry? (v.2)

☐ Yes ☐ No

5. Are you respectable? Do you handle yourself in an orderly and well-behaved manner, rather than being childish, ill mannered, and immature? (v. 2)

☐ Yes ☐ No

6. Are you given to hospitality? Are you willing to open your heart, home and material resources to others? Do you serve and minister to the needs of others on a regular basis? (v. 2)

☐ Yes ☐ No

7. Are you able to teach the Word to others? Do you look for and take advantage of opportunities to communicate biblical truth to those around you? (v. 2)

☐ Yes ☐ No

8. Do you exhibit self-control in matters of food and drink or in practices that could cause others to stumble? (v. 3)

☐ Yes ☐ No

9. Are you peaceable and non-combative rather than quick-tempered and argumentative? Are you able to deal with those who contradict you in a gentle, reasonable way? (v. 3)

☐ Yes ☐ No

10. Are you free from a contentious spirit? Are you "slow to anger" rather than quarrelsome? Do you seek to avoid strife? (v. 3)

☐ Yes ☐ No

11. Are you free from the love of money, covetousness, and greedy gain? Have you avoided undue entanglement in secular money affairs and over-interest in money, retirement, the things of this world? (v. 3)

☐ Yes ☐ No

12. Do you manage your own household well? Are your children faithful rather than rebellious toward God? Do you handle your children with dignity and in a respectable, commendable way that is an example to others? (v. 4)

☐ Yes ☐ No

13. Are you an established believer? Are you mature in the faith rather than a new convert? (v. 6)

☐ Yes ☐ No

14. Are you selfless rather than self-willed? Are you willing to yield your rights rather than insisting on getting your own way? (Titus 1:7)

☐ Yes ☐ No

15. Are you a lover of that which is good (i.e. good men, good things, good values, etc)? (Titus 1:8)

☐ Yes ☐ No

16. Are you just and fair in all your dealings? Do you have a genuine desire to do that which is right and honorable in the sight of others? (Titus 1:8)

☐ Yes ☐ No

17. Are you devout? Are you wholly devoted to Christ and willing to be set apart unto Him? (Titus 1:8)

☐ Yes ☐ No

18. Are you self-controlled? Are you letting Christ rule and reign over your life? Are you able to discipline yourself, apart from externally imposed disciplines? (Titus 1:8)

☐ Yes ☐ No

19. Are you an example of godliness in your speech? (v. 12)

☐ Yes ☐ No

20. Are you an example of godliness in your conduct? (v. 12)

❒ Yes ❒ No

21. Are you an example of godliness in your love? (v. 12)

❒ Yes ❒ No

22. Are you an example of godliness in your faith? (v. 12)

❒ Yes ❒ No

23. Are you an example of godliness in your purity? (v. 12)

❒ Yes ❒ No

24. Are you taking pains with, absorbed in, persevering, and making evident progress in the development of godly character? (v. 15ff)

❒ Yes ❒ No

25. Are you taking pains with, absorbed in, persevering, and making evident progress in the development of your teaching? (v. 15)

❒ Yes ❒ No

1 Timothy 5

26. Do you treat others with respect rather than reproving them sharply? (v. 1, 2)

❒ Yes ❒ No

27. Do you take care of the material and spiritual needs of your own household? (v. 8)

☐ Yes ☐ No

1 Timothy 6

28. Are you content with what God has provided? Do you see what God has provided as enough? (v. 6-10)

☐ Yes ☐ No

2 Timothy 1

29. Do you maintain a clear conscience? Are you consistently right before God and man? (v. 3; 1 Timothy 1:19)

☐ Yes ☐ No

30. Have you overcome a spirit of timidity or a man-fearing spirit? Are you unashamed of the Lord and the Lord's servants? (v. 7, 8)

☐ Yes ☐ No

2 Timothy 2

31. Are you personally involved in teaching faithful men who in turn can teach others? Do you exhibit a lifestyle of personal discipleship? (v. 2)

☐ Yes ☐ No

32. Are you willing to suffer hardship? Are you willing to do the will of God regardless of the cost? (v. 3)

☐ Yes ☐ No

33. Are you preoccupied with Christ rather than the things and interests of this world? Are your priorities aligned with those taught in God's Word? Do you have an eternal perspective? (v. 4)

☐ Yes ☐ No

34. Do you "compete according to the rules"? Do you order your life according to biblical principles? (v. 5)

☐ Yes ☐ No

35. Are you hard working and diligent? Are you willing to aggressively tackle any responsibility regardless of its difficulty? (v. 6)

☐ Yes ☐ No

36. Do you study the Word of God diligently and handle it accurately? (v. 15)

☐ Yes ☐ No

37. Do you avoid worldly and empty chatter? (v. 16)

☐ Yes ☐ No

38. Do you consistently cleanse yourself of any impurity of life? Do you flee youthful lusts, and are you pursuing righteousness, purity, and holiness?
(v. 21, 22)

☐ Yes ☐ No

39. Do you refuse foolish and ignorant speculations that produce quarrels? (v. 23)

☐ Yes ☐ No

40. Are you kind to all? (v. 24)

☐ Yes ☐ No

41. Are you patient when wronged? (v. 24)

☐ Yes ☐ No

42. Do you gently correct those who are in opposition to the truth? (v. 25)

☐ Yes ☐ No

2 Timothy 3

43. Do you have a godly perspective on the wickedness of the day in which we live? Do you see clearly the enemies that oppose the things of God? (v. 1-9)

☐ Yes ☐ No

44. Are you teachable? Do you follow the example of godly men? (v. 10)

☐ Yes ☐ No

45. Are you faithful in the study and application of the Word of God to equip yourself as a man of God? (v. 14-16)

☐ Yes ☐ No

2 Timothy 4

46. Do you proclaim consistently and faithfully the whole counsel of the Word?
(v. 2)

☐ Yes ☐ No

47. Are you ready to serve God in season and out of season (i.e. at all times, regardless of the circumstances)? (v. 2)

☐ Yes ☐ No

48. Are you willing to reprove and rebuke men? Are you unafraid to confront others who stand in opposition? Are you more interested in pleasing God than pleasing man? (v. 2)

☐ Yes ☐ No

49. Do you minister to others with great patience and biblical instruction? (v. 2)

☐ Yes ☐ No

50. Are you fulfilling faithfully the ministry that God has given you right where you are? (v. 4-8)

☐ Yes ☐ No

Obviously every man God uses contends with sin and weakness daily. Yet no man can willfully and consistently rebel against God and be the leader God wants him to be. Leadership without spirituality usually ends in a mere show of faked piety. Such leadership is not just neutral but damaging to the Body of Christ as it cools flames of passion for the Lord in other believers.

Has God shown you something about yourself you wish were not there? For rebellion and pretense there is only one course of action: repentance. Humble yourself and reject sin, despising it for the evil that it is. If you have sinned against others, confess your sin to as many as your sin or its effect has touched. And where you found weakness, renew spiritual disciplines. But in every consideration apply faith in God the Sanctifier. It is God who makes you holy and effective.

Memorize verses applicable to your need. Let God's Word search you daily. Ask for help from others who can hold you accountable and give you counsel. Aggressively cooperate with the Holy Spirit, the agent of change in your life. Trust God to broaden your leadership according to a growing foundation of true spirituality. And plead with God to keep you from ever being surface, vain, and useless as a leader. Ask God to make you a vessel fit for the Master's use.

"50 Marks of a Man of God" is available in booklet form at www.TruthInkPublications.com

APPENDIX B

STRATEGIC PLANNING

Strategic planning is an art and one of the great keys to good leadership. Many, many churches are floundering with little vision because the leaders don't understand this process.

Every pastor needs to learn how to take his team(s) through this process. It's part of his job as a good overseer. One of the best books on this subject is, *Masterplanning*, by Bobb Biehl. What follows is a modified plan of his approach. I am putting it in an illustrated form of a plan partially filled out by a Youth Pastor of a church so you can actually see how it functions.

In the annual process of the year, the church leadership team should spend time together seeking God's direction for the overarching theme or objective of the year. Perhaps it's evangelism or equipping that need to be highlighted that year. This should not be done to the exclusion of all the normal, working ministries of the church, but is the area that is going to be emphasized or developed. Think of it this way: "Where is the greatest area of need among our people and the people we are seeking to reach? What does God want us to emphasize this year? Family issues? Spiritual development? Evangelistic outreach? etc." This emphasis should be communicated to the staff and should be reflected in their individual annual strategic plan.

Once a staff member (the youth pastor in the following illustration) develops his individual plan, this should be reviewed and developed further with whoever directly supervises him until all the individual plans are finalized. Together, these plans will give you a working strategic plan for the year.

2008-2009 Strategic Plan

The Summit Church exists to cooperate with God in developing multiplying communities of fully devoted followers of Christ

Ministry: Youth Team
Leader: Jones

I. Mission:

(overall mission, never changes year to year)

II. Objectives, Goals and Strategies

- Objective (key areas of work to accomplish mission)
- Goals (specific, reachable, measurable desired outcomes for objectives)
- Strategies: (specific plans to accomplish goals)
- Dates: (target date for accomplishment
- Budget: (financial resources)

#	Objective	Goals	Strategy	Dates	Budget
1	Events	To Engage 500 students in large events	Mudbowl	9/1/09	$1000
			After game rallys	9/15; 9/27; 10/15; 10/23	500
2		To see 25 students come to know Christ personally	Winter retreat	2/12/09	500
3			Summer camp	6/15/09	3000
			Weekly gathering	Weekly	500
4	Large Group	To average 175 students in weekly worship gatherings	The Spot- high school worship	Wed p.m. weekly	$1000
5			Middle School worship	Wed p.m. weekly	$1000
7	Small Groups	To engage 175 students in 17 effective small groups	Small groups	Wed p.m. and various times	$500
8	Leadership Training	To effectively train an army of 35 youth leaders	Group leader training	Monthly training mtgs and retreat	$500
9		To train 3 interns and prepare them for youth ministry	Intern training	All year	$1000
10		To train 25 key student leaders	Student training weekends	10/12/08; 3/15/09	$500
11	Communication	To effectively communicate the ministry to our parents	Parent orientation	8/7/08	$50
12			Monthly parent letter	Monthly	$150
13			Quarterly communiqué	9/1; 12/1 3/1; 6/1	$100
15	Parent involvement	To directly engage 100 parents in student ministry at some level	The Spot- 10 parents	weekly	
16			Beach trip- 15 parents	Jun 17-23	

Other Writings by Bill Elliff

Forgiveness
Healing the Harbored
Hurts of your Heart

Everyman…
the Rescue

Lifting the Load
How to Gain and Maintain
a Clear Conscience

Turning the Tide
Having MORE Kids who
Follow Christ
(Holly Elliff with Bill Elliff)

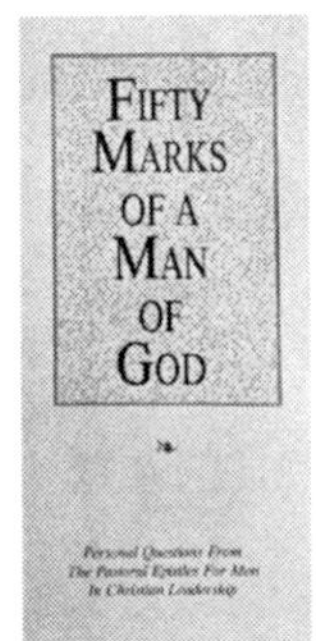

50 Marks of a
Man of God
Important questions
for those in
spiritual leadership

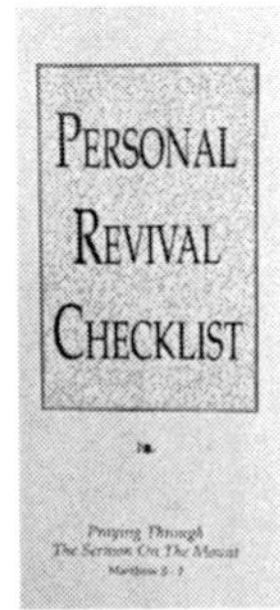

Personal Revival
Checklist

To order more copies of *Whitewater* or any of our other resources, contact TruthInkPublications.com. Bulk prices available upon request.

CPSIA information can be obtained at www.ICGtesting.com
233225LV00002B/2/P

9 780615 403083